MW00778927

TOWARD A LATINO/A
BIBLICAL INTERPRETATION

RESOURCES FOR BIBLICAL STUDY

Editor
Tom Thatcher, New Testament

Number 91

TOWARD A LATINO/A
BIBLICAL INTERPRETATION

Francisco Lozada Jr.

SBL PRESS

 **PRESS**

Atlanta

Copyright © 2017 by Francisco Lozada Jr.

All rights reserved. No part of this work may be reproduced or transmitted in any form or by any means, electronic or mechanical, including photocopying and recording, or by means of any information storage or retrieval system, except as may be expressly permitted by the 1976 Copyright Act or in writing from the publisher. Requests for permission should be addressed in writing to the Rights and Permissions Office, SBL Press, 825 Houston Mill Road, Atlanta, GA 30329 USA.

Library of Congress Cataloging-in-Publication Data

Names: Lozada, Francisco, 1965– author.
Title: Toward a Latino/a biblical interpretation / by Francisco Lozada Jr.
Other titles: Toward a Latino biblical interpretation | Toward a Latina biblical interpretation
Description: Atlanta : SBL Press, [2017] | Series: Resources for biblical study ; Number 91 | Includes bibliographical references and index.
Identifiers: LCCN 2017033560 (print) | LCCN 2017034230 (ebook) | ISBN 9780884142690 (ebook) | ISBN 9781628372007 (pbk. : alk. paper) | ISBN 9780884142706 (hardcover : alk. paper)
Subjects: LCSH: Bible. New Testament—Criticism, interpretation, etc. | Bible. New Testament—Criticism, interpretation, etc.—Latin America.
Classification: LCC BS2361.3 (ebook) | LCC BS2361.3 .L69 2017 (print) | DDC 220.6089/68—dc23
LC record available at https://lccn.loc.gov/2017033560

Printed on acid-free paper.

CONTENTS

Acknowledgments

I would like to thank my colleagues at Brite Divinity School for their support and encouragement; Cathy L. Roan, PhD, for her close reading of the volume; and Alvin Rapien, my student assistant, for his help in providing a student's perspective. I especially want to thank my family (Wendi, Nico, and Ana) for their patience and especially, my parents, Francisco and Fidela Lozada, for passing down their steadfast love of our culture. It is to my parents that I dedicate this volume.

1

Introduction: Theorizing Latino/a Biblical Interpretation

Latino/a[1] biblical interpretation does not come out of nowhere. In a way, Latino/a biblical interpretation presupposes the history of biblical interpretation and both reacts to and builds upon this history. Latino/a biblical interpretation is part of the history of biblical interpretation. Without it, the history of biblical interpretation is incomplete. This volume aims to contribute to this history by discussing various ways Latino/a biblical interpretation has been practiced and conceived of as part of the history of biblical interpretation.

A maxim I occasionally employ in class is "how one interprets a text (ancient or modern) influences how one sees another and treats another in the present world." This is why interpretation is important and why it is important to know. By studying Latino/a biblical hermeneutics or interpretation,[2] one may gain a fuller understanding of Latinos/as in

---

1. The nomenclature *Latino/a* aims to be inclusive of both men and women as well as to signify the problematics of gender and sexuality formations along a binary system. The nomenclature *Latinx* has also recently been employed in discourse and writings aimed at capturing all of the above problematics.

2. First, I am using hermeneutics and interpretation synonymously. Second, the term *hermeneutics* can be understood in many different ways. In this volume, it is understood as the examination of the general principles underlying interpretation (see, e.g., Emilio Betti), but it is also seen as the exploration of those factors involved in interpretative process (see, e.g., Hans-Georg Gadamer). Thus, in this volume, I am less concerned about direct engagement with the philosophical tradition and more interested in drawing on the history of hermeneutics tradition to inform my understanding of Latino/a biblical interpretation. To explore different understandings of hermeneutics, see Richard E. Palmer, *Hermeneutics: Interpretation Theory in Schleiermacher, Dilthey, Heidegger, and Gadamer*, Northwestern

general and a better understanding of the character of Latino/a interpretation, which fosters, I believe, an open-mindedness and receptiveness toward difference. In fact, the study of hermeneutics or interpretation, such as minoritized hermeneutics,[3] nurtures respect and understanding for the Other[4] without undermining one's convictions in how he or she (they) might read and receive the biblical tradition. In short, it teaches all how to live creatively with difference in times when difference is feared and rebuked. The study of hermeneutics, such as Latino/a biblical interpretation, does so by understanding the diverse motivations and journeys Latinos/as take that have led them in the first place to read in the fashion(s) that they have chosen.[5] It does so by teaching how one comes to know, how one thinks, and how one legitimates one's claims. By reading Latino/a hermeneutics sympathetically, with an open outlook, Latino/a interpretation, like many other perspectives, teaches how Latinos/as read, apply, and respond to texts.[6] Yet these intercultural contributions that Latino/a biblical interpretation make are not the only reasons why Latino/a biblical interpretation is important.

For many Latino/a biblical interpreters, as with other marginalized groups, entrance to university and theological studies also brings access to the discipline of biblical interpretation. It is well documented now that Latinos/as are recent participants in the various scholarly guilds and in colleges, universities, and theological/seminary institutions. With their presence, for many, come new questions and new ways of seeing text. The presence of Latino/a biblical interpreters thus challenges the way bibli-

---

University Studies in Phenomenology and Existential Philosophy (Evanston, IL: Northwestern University Press, 1969).

3. For an illustrative use of minoritized criticism, see Randall C. Bailey, Tat-Siong Benny Liew, and Fernando F. Segovia, eds., *They Were All Together in One Place? Toward Minority Biblical Criticism*, SemeiaSt 57 (Atlanta: Society of Biblical Literature, 2009).

4. The term *Other* is used broadly to refer to those whose identities or characteristics that are deemed inferior by dominant groups. See Stephen Castles and Mark J. Miller, *The Age of Migration: International Population Movements in the Modern World*, 4th ed. (New York: Guilford, 2009), 35.

5. See Anthony C. Thiselton, *Hermeneutics: An Introduction* (Grand Rapids: Eerdmans, 2009), 5–15. Thiselton does a very good job in discussing the benefits of studying hermeneutics.

6. Ibid., 1.

cal interpretation has been done and contributes to the way the field is practiced. Their unique and vastly diverse social and community experiences, brought to bear on interpretation, keep the construct Latino/a unstable—rarely fixed but always fluid. In a way, what one is witnessing with the arrival of Latinos/as is the democratization of the academy, and it is not necessarily one of assimilation where Latinos/as may enter on the condition that they adhere to the "exegetical" rules constructed by the dominant group—though this does occur. The arrival is also one of integration, where one may participate in the academy and maintain or construct a different way of reading critically.[7] This is not a far cry from how society today, via some political leaders in the United States, calls on newly arrived migrants or minoritized groups to adhere to the US "way of life" if they wish to be members of the US community. However, Latino/a biblical interpretation is more reflective of a multicultural-integrative model of community in the sense that Latinos/as enter the guild with the intention of not giving up their distinctive identities but rather using them to participate in and widen the existing boundaries on how to do biblical interpretation. This also is not a far cry away from how society today, via some political leaders, calls on society to embrace diversity, allowing difference to maintain their distinctive cultures in the community while adhering to certain values and laws. At the same time, there are some Latinos/as who even transcend national boundaries in the practice of interpretation, leading them to multiple forms of belonging. This is also reflected in many Latinos/as holding onto two (sometimes conflicting) political identities: one here in the United States and another, for example, in Latin America.[8] This is a result, I believe, of racialization and globaliza-

---

7. One may argue that by maintaining presence in an academy (i.e., the Society of Biblical Literature) where the ethos (scientific) still does not welcome difference is reifying such an ethos. Though this line of thinking has merit, another line of thinking suggests that by remaining in such an academy, one's presence can transform it from within. For a discussion of this topic, see Elisabeth Schüssler Fiorenza and Kent H. Richards, eds., *Transforming Graduate Biblical Education: Ethos and Discipline*, GPBS 10 (Atlanta: Society of Biblical Literature, 2010).

8. See Alejandro F. Botta, "What Does It Mean to Be a Latino Biblical Critic? A Brief Essay," in *Latino/a Biblical Hermeneutics: Problematics, Objectives, Strategies*, ed. Francisco Lozada Jr. and Fernando F. Segovia, SemeiaSt 68 (Atlanta: SBL Press, 2014), 107–19; Jacqueline M. Hidalgo, "Reading from No Place: Toward a Hybrid and Ambivalent Study," in Lozada and Segovia, *Latino/a Biblical*

tion of the field of biblical interpretation, which constructs an either/or identification system.

Another explanation for the emergence of Latino/a biblical interpretation, as I see it, is because biblical interpretation as it had been practiced and conceived no longer held or only partially held any future for Latinos/as. In other words, it did not address the concerns or issues that many Latinos/as in the United States were confronting on a daily basis. Much of biblical interpretation was simply a reading that reflected the *art of exegesis*: how best to practice and use the tools of modern biblical criticism. It served the interest primarily of the academy and academic institutions and the interpreters who espoused the scientific principles of positivism, objectivity, and universalism.[9] Interpreters often hide behind a scientific mask of neutrality that colors them as omniscient authorities about the world behind the text and quenches the readers' thirst to know what the text (and God) really means.[10] The art of exegesis also served, for some, the interest of ecclesial authority, extracting theological principles through historical excavation in order to apply them to believers and reify notions of biblical authority and ecclesial authority. For many Latinos/as, the vested interests of the academy, academia, interpreters, and ecclesial authorities who espoused the art of exegesis (as highly ideological as all readings) served the interest of those in power. This type of interpretation did not serve the well-being of the Latino/a community or any groups that were marginalized or oppressed across the globe.[11] Thus, Latino/a biblical interpretation contributes to the development of biblical interpretation by

---

Hermeneutics, 165–86; Osvaldo D. Vena, "El Sur También Existe: A Proposal for Dialogue between Latin American and Latino/a Hermeneutics," in Lozada and Segovia, *Latino/a Biblical Hermeneutics*, 297–319.

9. To understand the development of objectivity in the sciences, see Lorraine Daston and Peter Galison, *Objectivity* (New York: Zone, 2010).

10. See Mary Ann Tolbert, "Writing History, Writing Culture, Writing Ourselves," in *Soundings in Cultural Criticism: Perspectives and Methods in Culture, Power, and Identity in the New Testament*, ed. Francisco Lozada Jr. and Greg Carey, Soundings (Minneapolis: Fortress, 2013), 17–30. Tolbert concisely and perspicaciously explores the epistemological issues related to doing biblical interpretation in a postmodern context.

11. For an excellent ethnographic analysis of how Latinos/as employ the scriptures at the "popular" level, see Efrain Agosto, "Reading the Word in America: US Latino/a Religious Communities and Their Scriptures," in *MisReading America:*

establishing a bridge (not a wall) between opposing viewpoints and prac-tices, not necessarily conforming to the dominant way of doing biblical interpretation but respecting the other way, even employing its tools, in the quest to understand critically what exactly one is doing when a text is read, understood, or engaged.

A final reason why Latino/a interpretation emerged has to do with its turn toward the community as an important component in the interpre-tative process. This focus forced Latinos/as out of the shadows to share critically the interests that they brought to bear to the text. This "coming out" encouraged readers (Latinos/as) to learn or rediscover their history (as well as that of indigenous and African peoples), culture, languages, religions, sexualities, gender, races/ethnicities, classes, disabilities/abili-ties, to name just a few. It is a process of being "born anew," if you will, and professing their identity to the public. It is an exercise in critical honesty. At the same time, Latino/a interpretation has been criticized by many for only speaking to a Latino/a audience and thus "navel gazing," and indeed the interpretation can be problematic if identity is not critically examined (not romanticized) as part of the interpretative process. But at the same time, such criticism is rarely leveled against Anglo-American writings. In other words, do not Latino/a readers have to assimilate another world (e.g., US Anglo-American writers) to grasp the meanings of the text? For me to understand Rudolf Bultmann, I need to understand his German context, no? This issue of writing to your audience surely is a question that needs further exploration in Latino/a biblical interpretation. In chapter 4 I subtly address this question by shifting focus away from identity toward an issue that is common not just in the Latino/a community but also in many other communities—recognition and hospitality. I do so intentionally to reflect, for myself, on how I would react to such a move. It appears to me that, in this ever-changing globalized world, a primary goal of Latino/a biblical interpretation ought to be for it to be seen as an equal yet distinct interpretation to be studied and understood, an interpretation that con-tributes not only to its own community but beyond.

Another hermeneutical point I wish to make relates to the role of understanding in Latino/a biblical interpretation. All of the following

---

Scriptures and Difference, ed. Vincent L. Wimbush with Lalruatkima and Melissa Renee Reid (Oxford: Oxford University Press, 2010), 117–64.

chapters aim to explore the text in order to promote understanding both of the text and of the interpreter. Understanding is an activity.[12] Taking this idea and applying it to Latino/a biblical interpretation, understanding is the connecting of the Latino/a experience of reality with the text. Latinos/as translate and analyze a text to understand the past, present, and future. It is an activity because it translates the past into the present in light of the future—not just for Latinos/as but for all. In bringing the past into the present in light of the future, understanding produces meaning and discloses the interpreter (or reader) as an active participant in the activity of bringing experience and text together. Thus, when Latino/a biblical interpreters embark on this move toward understanding as activity, they concretize the text through the use of language, mediating the past and the future in their present interpretation. This activity is like a dialogue in which both the interpreter and the text are in conversation in order to understand the other and in order for the interpreter to understand oneself or one's community. Some particular approaches of Latino/a biblical interpretation take different paths, but they all work with a notion of the text not as static but rather as a living text that still bears some relevance (sometimes more than others) to the one interpreting it. It is a dynamic activity with real-life consequences affecting Latinos/as' community, identification, and representation. In the nascent history of Latino/a biblical interpretation, Latinos/as have engaged in interpretation to look for the meaning of texts in dialogue with Latino/a experience; they employ texts seeking an understanding of their Latino/a interpretation as it seeks authenticity in their world; and they examine texts to understand the meaning of being Latino/a. In short, Latino/a biblical interpretation is an activity on all fronts of belonging—similar to what many marginalized groups are seeking in the United States today.

Construing Latino/a Biblical Hermeneutics and Interpretation

Part of theorizing Latino/a biblical interpretation entails understanding those aspects of the approach that might not receive attention, namely,

---

12. See David E. Klemm, introduction to *The Interpretation of Texts*, vol. 1 of *Hermeneutical Inquiry*, AARSR 43 (Atlanta: Scholars Press, 1986), 1–54. Klemm has strongly informed my thinking on this point.

contextualization, nature of texts, and community. Critical reflection on these aspects allows readers to see the elements that contribute to the development of a Latino/a biblical approach. This, of course, helps readers become more intimate with the approach in general and with the strategies in particular, and it introduces them to topics rarely nuanced or discussed. In this volume, I explore these three aspects—contextualization, nature of texts, community—of Latino/a biblical interpretation. To construe Latino/a biblical interpretation in such a way contributes to a better understanding of the tactics or moves that regularly get overlooked in this particular approach.[13]

---

13. Works that bear directly on the discussion here and throughout the volume include: Fernando F. Segovia, "Hispanic American Theology and the Bible: Effective Weapon and Faithful Ally," in *We Are a People! Initiatives in Hispanic American Theology*, ed. Roberto S. Goizueta (Minneapolis: Fortress, 1992), 21–49; Segovia, "Toward Latino/a American Biblical Criticism: Latin(o/a)ness as Problematic," in Bailey, Liew, and Segovia, *They Were all Together*, 193–223; Jean-Pierre Ruiz, *Readings from the Edges: The Bible and People on the Move*, Studies in Latino/a Catholicism (Maryknoll, NY: Orbis Books, 2011); Ruiz, "The Bible and Latino/a Theology," in *The Wiley Blackwell Companion to Latino/a Theology*, ed. Orlando O. Espín (Malden, MA: Wiley-Blackwell, 2015), 111–27; Efraín Agosto, "Sola Scriptura and Latino/a Protestant Hermeneutics: An Exploration," in *Building Bridges, Doing Justice: Constructing a Latino/a Ecumenical Theology*, ed. Orlando O. Espín (Maryknoll, NY: Orbis Books, 2009), 69–87; David Sánchez, *From Patmos to the Barrio: Subverting Imperial Myths* (Minneapolis: Fortress, 2008); Jacqueline M. Hidalgo, *Revelation in Aztlán: Scriptures, Utopias, and the Chicano Movement*, The Bible and Cultural Studies (New York: Palgrave Macmillan, 2016). Other works by theologians employing the biblical text that also bear peripherally on the discussion here include: Virgilio Elizondo, *Galilean Journey: The Mexican-American Promise* (Maryknoll, NY: Orbis Books, 1983); Justo L. González, *Santa Biblia: The Bible through Hispanic Eyes* (Nashville: Abingdon, 1996); Harold J. Recinos, *Good News from the Barrio: Prophetic Witness for the Church* (Louisville: Westminster John Knox, 2006); Daisy L. Machado, "The Unnamed Woman: Justice, Feminists, and the Undocumented Woman," in *A Reader in Latina Feminist Theology: Religion and Justice*, ed. María Pilar Aquino, Daisy L. Machado, and Jeanette Rodríguez (Austin: University of Texas Press, 2002), 161–76. Other studies that bear indirectly on the discussion here include: Rudy V. Busto, "'It Really Resembled an Earthly Paradise': Reading Motolinía's Account of the Caída de nuestros primeros padres," *BibInt* 2 (1994): 111–37; Cristina García-Alfonso, "El silencio del cuerpo: La historia de Tamar," in *Camino a Emaús: Compartiendo el ministerio de Jesús*, ed. Ada María Isasi-Díaz, Timoteo Matovina, and Nina M. Torres-Vidal

Contextualization

A primary facet of Latino/a biblical interpreters is contextualization, that is, the contextualization of the text under study, the interpreter, and readings of a text or its readers. Regarding the text under study, interpreters are interested in understanding the context behind the text, namely, its sociohistorical context. To apply contextualization to the interpreter is not an ephemeral gesture to delineating the social factors of one's identity; rather it is a critical and developed examination of the interpreter's context and how that context influences the reading of a text or a community. This critical analysis also extends to readings of a text across communities and across times and places. At times, the context of the text is given more attention, and, at other times, the context of the reader (or readings) is given more attention.

For those interested in the production of the text, the context of the sociohistorical world is the mode of entry in one's interpretative task. Attention is given to what the text meant to the authors in question in their relationships with their intended readers. Some might draw on philology or textual criticism in order to provide a grammatical or transmission history of the text that they are studying, but they do not necessarily do this reconstruction under the cloak of neutral objectivity. Latino/a biblical interpreters also study the genre of the documents and the language and style that its authors used. Some do bear in mind the historical setting in which the author wrote (general historical information), such as the ancient Near East or Greco-Roman world; Judaism and/or the Roman Empire, with all its expressions at various periods of time; and the emerging "Christian" community, with its various strands of tradition. The general aim here is to connect the text under study with the life of the community out of which the text came in order to relate it to the histori-

---

(Minneapolis: Fortress, 2002), 31–42; Pablo Jiménez, "In Search of a Hispanic Model of Biblical Interpretation," *JHLT* 3 (1995): 66–79; Maricel Mena-López, "Because of an Ethiopian Woman: Reflections on Race, Gender, and Religion in the Biblical World," in *Feminist Intercultural Theology: Latina Explorations for a Just World*, ed. María Pilar Aquino and Maria José Rosado-Nunes, Studies in Latino/a Catholicism (Maryknoll, NY: Orbis Books, 2007), 145–65; Gilbert C. Romero, *Hispanic Devotional Piety: Tracing Biblical Roots* (Maryknoll, NY: Orbis Books, 1991). Other studies are noted throughout the volume.

cal or social realities of the Latino/a community, despite the assertion that the sources of antiquity, especially for early Christian studies, are ambiguous and scarce.[14] All of this is to say that Latino/a biblical interpreters are fully aware that the text under study is historically conditioned in various ways by the world and communities surrounding it. What distinguishes Latino/a biblical interpreters hermeneutically from the dominant objective-neutral approach of historical reconstruction is a different notion of objectivity; that is, a notion of objectivity that is not based on one correct meaning, but rather one that sees objectivity as the compilation of multiple meanings of a text. In this case, arriving at a conclusive reading of a text for all (including the Latino/a community) is never achieved, as I see it. One may reach a conclusive reading of a text temporarily for a particular community, but interpretation or meaning is not something one could store in a museum for perpetuity. In this two-step process of interpretation, the interpreter chooses, therefore, to do the historical reconstruction of a text first and then apply this reconstructed work to his or her (their) context. Those Latino/a interpreters who choose this route are (or might be) working with an assumption that one should keep close to the socially constructed intended meaning of a text while letting the present context of the interpreter tangentially inform the interpretative process.

But Latino/a biblical interpreters are also fully aware that they themselves (as interpreters) are also historically conditioned in various ways by the world and communities surrounding them. They no longer see themselves as scientists whose reconstructions of history or the narrative text mirror reality, precisely or approximately, giving the impression of an all-knowing scholar (the mask of omniscience).[15] Instead, Latino/a interpreters see their analysis and thus interpretations as constructions; that is, they are fully aware that interpretation is a subjective enterprise—a critical subjective enterprise that takes seriously the identity of the interpreter and text. Thus, by providing an analysis of the context of the interpreter or his or her (their) community, the interpreter sees him or herself (themselves) in general as a theologian and/or cultural critic—ideologically or politically—who shapes how readers see the world behind, in, and in front

---

14. See Tolbert, "Writing History, Writing Culture, Writing Ourselves," 20. She does not make the same claim for Hebrew Bible studies, which can draw from a larger mass of sources.

15. See ibid., 24. See also Daston and Galison, *Objectivity*, 36–39.

of the text.[16] According to this view of the role of the interpreter—which differs both from those who espouse an objective-neutral way of reading and from those who practice biblical interpretation in the traditional way—the interpreter engages the process of interpretation in order to better serve the community in the various ways interpreters deem fit. Thus this question of the role of the interpreter and contextualization has not disappeared in the last thirty years or so for the many engaged in the field of Latino/a biblical interpretation. In fact, the question is present in every chapter in this volume through the analysis of the Latino/a community in its plurality and also through an examination of the interpreter or his or her (their) subjectivity. Thus, no suppression of subjectivity exists in this volume, nor is the mode of entry into interpretation one that begins with text per se. Subjectivity is always intrinsic to the interpretative process, as philosophical hermeneutics have argued.[17] However, contextualizing the interpreter or the interpreter's community does run the risk of leaving a strong imprint on the interpretation of a text. Just like a metacritique ought to be applied to the dominant and traditional ways of doing biblical interpretation, a metacritique ought to be subjected to minoritized and nontraditional ways of doing interpretation as well.

This turn toward the contextualization of the interpreter in Latino/a biblical interpretation is not unique. One only has to understand its influences, directly and indirectly, to understand what Latino/a biblical interpretation is aiming to do by turning its attention to the role of the interpreter. Philosophically, Latino/a biblical interpretation is predisposed to the contributions of ideological hermeneutics with its attention toward understanding how texts and readers are shaped by their vested interests (e.g., Hans-Georg Gadamer, Paul Ricoeur, Jürgen Habermas).[18]

---

16. See Fernando F. Segovia, "Poetics of Minority Biblical Criticism: Identification and Theorization," in *Prejudice and Christian Beginnings: Investigating Race, Gender, and Ethnicity in Early Christian Studies*, ed. Laura Nasrallah and Elisabeth Schüssler Fiorenza (Minneapolis: Fortress, 2009), 302.

17. See Palmer, *Hermeneutics*, 194–217. Here I am particularly referring to the thinking of Gadamer.

18. Hans-Georg Gadamer, "The Universality of the Hermeneutical Problem," ed. and trans. David Linge, in Klemm, *Interpretation of Texts*, 179–89; Paul Ricoeur, "Existence and Hermeneutics," ed. Don Ihde, trans. Kathleen McLaughlin, in *The Interpretation of Existence*, vol. 2 of *Hermeneutical Inquiry*, ed. David E. Klemm, AARSR 44 (Atlanta: Scholars Press, 1986), 185–202; Jürgen Habermas,

Theologically, Latin American liberation hermeneutics and its position that understanding is related to life and life in community influences Latino/a biblical interpretation.[19] Culturally, feminist/*mujerista* and other minoritized hermeneutics, with their suspicion of the power of language and tradition as instruments of oppression, have left their fingerprints on the identity of Latino/a biblical interpretation.[20] Hence, one can find traces of all these affiliations, and more, in Latino/a biblical interpretation's focus on the role of the interpreter in shaping understanding.

What Latino/a biblical interpretation does with all these influences is to thematize the role of context in the interpretative process. It is not simply about delimiting one's context, but it is also about demonstrating the process in such a way that the interpreter encounters or engages the text's meaning in relation to his or her (their) community's or own interest. What the interpreter is engaging is not the intent of the author per se (at least for me) but the representational world opened up by the language of the text.[21] This aim to demonstrate how context plays a role in interpretation is also reflected in all the chapters in this volume. Thus the reading or the engagement of a text leads to a particular reading of a text via various approaches that intends to introduce a particular interpretation, not in a purely subjective way, but one strongly informed by the contextualization

---

"Towards a Theory of Communicative Competence," in Klemm, *Interpretation of Existence*, 209–34.

19. E.g., Leonardo Boff, *Jesus Christ Liberator: A Critical Christology for Our Time* (Maryknoll, NY: Orbis Books, 1978); Elsa Tamez, *The Amnesty of Grace: Justification by Faith from a Latin American Perspective*, trans. Sharon H. Ringe (Nashville: Abingdon, 1993); Jon Sobrino, *Jesus the Liberator: A Historical-Theological Reading of Jesus of Nazareth* (Maryknoll, NY: Orbis Books, 1994).

20. E.g., María Pilar Aquino, *Our Cry for Life: Feminist Theology from Latin America*, trans. Dinah Livingstone (Maryknoll, NY: Orbis Books, 1993); Ada María Isasi-Díaz, *Mujerista Theology: A Theology for the Twenty-First Century* (Maryknoll, NY: Orbis Books, 1996); Elisabeth Schüssler Fiorenza, *Jesus and the Politics of Interpretation* (New York: Continuum, 2000); Musa W. Dube, *Postcolonial Feminist Interpretation of the Bible* (St. Louis, MO: Chalice, 2000); Tat-Siong Benny Liew, *What Is Asian American Biblical Hermeneutics? Reading the New Testament*, Intersections: Asian and Pacific American Transcultural Studies (Honolulu: University of Hawai'i Press, 2007); Cain Hope Felder, ed., *Stony the Road We Trod: African American Biblical Interpretation* (Minneapolis: Fortress, 1991).

21. Thiselton, *Hermeneutics*, 228–54.

of the interpreter and the text by way of both components' history or literary representation.

Nature of Texts

Latino/a biblical interpretation insists that choosing an approach is essential for any critical interpretation of texts. All possible methods and theories available to Latino/a biblical interpreters may be applied to the biblical tradition and its reception. Latino/a biblical interpretation is not simply a matter of studying the writings of the Hebrew Bible or New Testament; it can also involve coordinating the Hebrew Bible with the New Testament; studying other readings (popular, ecclesial, or academic) of the biblical tradition; and studying how the Bible has been employed, consumed, and received by Latino/a communities. Thus, the scope of Latino/a interpretation is broad and not restricted to the exegesis of specific texts; it uses all sorts of reading strategies to study the biblical tradition (as this volume does).

For many Latino/a biblical interpreters this biblical tradition is Scripture—namely, authoritative, divinely inspired, and revelatory. These texts serve as witnesses to the Christian church and its tradition. The terms *authoritative, inspired,* and *revelation* may be understood in various ways, but they all influence Christian self-understanding. However, not all Latino/a biblical interpreters are Christian, and not all would espouse such theological assumptions. Some may see biblical texts not as Scripture (in uppercase), as it has been traditionally conceived, but rather as scripture (in lowercase) in the sense that it has an imperialist agenda and must employ, therefore, secular criticism.[22] Others may see biblical texts as scripture (in lowercase) with an ideological or theological agenda participating in the writing of history, writing narrative, writing Latino/a culture, and writing Latino/a(ness). The latter position is reflected in this volume. This is not to say that the text or scripture has no authority, but rather, such notions of authority move away from its author, content, or concepts and closer to the semantic representation that the engagement between interpreter and text constructs based on various criteria, such as the liberation of all of God's people. In this volume, particularly in the

---

22. See Hector Avalos, "Rethinking Latino Hermeneutics: An Atheist Perspective," in Lozada and Segovia, *Latino/a Biblical Hermeneutics,* 59–72.

fourth chapter, recognition and hospitality operate in the *authorization* of interpretation. This notion of authorization is not based on a scientific process of interpretation nor one ensured by a particular person or institution in a universal way but is instead based on an ethical criterion (transformation and liberation, in my case) that is constantly confronted to avoid a universal ethics. Authorization is a process that involves a collective experience that includes many influences—such as the interpreter, text, and community—in the determination of a text's relevance for a community. Since Scripture/scripture is a public, theological document, Latino/a biblical interpreters and others must participate in its interpretation, otherwise the rules of interpretation will be written without them (as they have been), thus marginalizing the collective identity of Latinos/as as objects rather than as subjects capable of translating, explaining, and proclaiming who they are and how and why they interpret.

Community

Another element of Latino/a biblical interpretation sees hermeneutic understanding as a transformative or liberative experience aimed at the Latino/a community and beyond.[23] It is a hermeneutic that does not try to argue for a single "way of life" but rather understands that the very encounter with texts has already changed the collective identity of Latinos/as, as any encounter with another community would do. It is not a one-sided assimilation process but rather a process that integrates other perspectives. As Latino/a biblical hermeneutics continues to develop, understanding the realities reflective of its community will serve to continue the hermeneutics' tradition of understanding the world and Latinos/as themselves. Latino/a biblical interpretation is a perfect antidote to the

---

23. Latino/a biblical interpreters' concern for how texts affect their community can, perhaps, trace its roots to those early Jewish and Christian interpreters known as part of the Alexandrian approach or allegorical method (e.g., Philo, Clement, and Origen) who also asked questions about the effect of texts upon its hearers and readers. See Robert M. Grant with David Tracy, *A Short History of the Interpretation of the Bible*, 2nd ed. (Philadelphia: Fortress, 1984), 52–62. See also Frances M. Young, *Biblical Exegesis and the Formation of the Christian Culture* (Grand Rapids: Baker Academic, 1997), 161–85.

fear of difference because it encourages conversation among different identities and communities.

Although the Latino/a community is not a homogeneous entity, both scholarship in general and even this volume sometimes treat it in a universalizing fashion. The Latino/a community thus exists at once both together and apart, as a single entity and as individual parts.[24] It is a complex community and perhaps even an imagined one, as I myself sometimes treat it in this volume. When such a construct (i.e., community) is accepted without critical reflection, the community remains in a static state, with certain individuals thinking of themselves as "authentic" while all others are excluded.[25] This is quite evident not only among the Latino/a community but in many other communities as well. In other words, this line of thinking resists changes to its understood authenticity or identity.[26] With regard to its use of community, this volume seeks to adopt a reflected position where individuals, including myself, resist any notion of an authentic community, that is, where identity mirrors the unreflected understanding of community. This volume treats community more fluidly, where Latino/a identity is always transforming, demanding a better life for itself.[27] For me, community is better understood as the various Latino/a identities that make up a community (a fluid understanding), as opposed to a community made up of selected identities (a static understanding).

Thus, Latino/a biblical interpretation, as I see it, and as I suggest throughout the volume, is about recognition. In other words, collectively and presently, Latino/a biblical interpretation leans toward understanding community as identity/belongingness, which, in effect, influences the writing and interpretation of Latino/a biblical interpretation.

Latino/a biblical interpretation aims to be recognized as equal to other forms of interpretation, yet it remains distinct by virtue of offering interpretation to both text and context without excluding other readings

24. See Tony Blackshaw, *Key Concepts in Community Studies*, SAGE Key Concepts (London: Sage, 2010), 32. Blackshaw provides an excellent critical evaluation of community, delineating it along six key concepts (theory, method, place, identity/belonging, ideology, and policy and practice).
25. Ibid., 12.
26. Ibid., 12 n. 1.
27. Ibid., 13–14.

of both text and context. Latino/a biblical interpretation is distinctive (identity) in the sense that it is different from other expressions of interpretation over time. At the same time, Latino/a biblical interpretation is constructed alongside and in relation to other expressions of interpretation (belongingness).[28] Latino/a biblical interpretation, as I will put forward in the following chapter, sees itself not so much as something fixed as something in flux. In other words, Latino/a biblical interpretation is a project that is constantly worked on and redefined in relation to other cultural expressions of interpretation. It tries to establish its presence in order to belong and, at the same time, attempts to preserve (for better or worse) its identity as a means to allow Latinos/as space and rhetoric to understand themselves in relation to understanding others. The community's notion of identity/belongingness surely informs Latino/a biblical interpretation's fixed and fluid distinctiveness. This depiction, it is important to note, aims to persuade *all readers* and not just Latinos/as to empathize with Latino/a biblical interpretations, drawing upon what we all have in common, so that we could extend this understanding to all other cultural identities and interpretations.[29] In this way, this study can be helpful in getting others to recognize (along the lines of epistemology and representation) Latino/a biblical interpretation as equal and distinct, worthy of study and understanding in its own right. By demonstrating or illustrating different reading strategies reflected in Latino/a biblical interpretation in the following chapters, readers are more likely to see the similarities between Latino/a biblical interpretation (and Latinos/as themselves) and other expressions of interpretation, which could lead to alliances rather than divisions.

A Look Ahead

This volume consists of five chapters beyond this introduction: the core, chapters 3–5, illustrates three different ways Latinos/as have engaged Latino/a biblical interpretation, and chapter 6 takes up the conditions needed to do Latino/a biblical interpretation. It is essential to note that

---

28. Ibid., 113.
29. Ibid., 114.

the applied readings (chs. 3–5) are how I see Latino/a biblical scholars practicing; more importantly, they do not designate a typology, nor are these three representative readings exhaustive of the group. As I mentioned above, Latino/a biblical interpretation is a project. Thus these three applications of Latino/a biblical interpretation are meant to be pedagogical in depicting the diverse ways Latino/a biblical interpretation can be construed, keeping in mind that in reality all three strategies draw from one another, depending on the aims of various interpreters.

Chapter 2, "Toward Latino/a Biblical Studies: Foregrounding Identities and Transforming Communities," aims to address the nature and identity of Latino/a biblical interpretation. It is meant to be a perspective that takes seriously its key components (Latino/a, biblical, interpretation) in order to arrive at some understanding of what Latino/a biblical interpretation tries to do and why it does what it does.

Chapter 3, "Journey and the Fourth Gospel: A Correlation Strategy," begins with a reading of the plot of the Fourth Gospel employing a strategy of correlation. Such an approach aims to show a relationship between the world of the interpreter and the world (in this case the narrative world) of the text. In this chapter I endeavor to draw on the experience of journey—not from my own experience but from my parents' experience as migrants and the experiences of many other Latino/a migrants in the United States. This effort is important because it seeks to help readers understand what migrants experience during journeys. I thus briefly discuss common aspects of this experience, then bring this experience to bear on a narrative reading of the plot of the Fourth Gospel. I suspend the limitations of such of an approach for the most part,[30] because it does have value in expanding the narrative world of the Fourth Gospel. In a way, the

---

30. A significant drawback in any attempt to bring identity to bear upon interpretation is the fixing of identity ontologically, which makes it difficult for other narratives to offer a competing narrative about that identity. However, I believe, at the moment, that as long as understanding others and ourselves is an important part of interpretation, a move toward the contextualization of the interpreter outweighs the exclusion of such a hermeneutical step. This limitation is also reflected in the other two strategies I employ in the following chapters, not to mention the traditional criticism that contextualization runs the risk of reading present reality into an ancient text; that is, assimilating another meaning to the text.

critical correlation approach heightens the point that all interpretation is anchored by contextualization.[31]

Chapter 4, "Matthew 6:9b–13 (The Lord's Prayer): A Dialogical Strategy," explores a second interpretive move, what I call a dialogical approach. Similar to the correlation approach in that both aim to fuse two separate worlds, the dialogical approach functions more like a conversation—a conversation between two components about an identity marker both share. The text under study is Matthew's Lord's Prayer (6:9b–11), and I take up the conversation of language, translation, and interpretation. On one side is the linguistic identity of the interpreter himself (me but similar to others who navigate through linguistic worlds); on the other is the text's interpretative history. This dialectical approach, I believe, advances a conversation in order to learn about the reader and the text, with the hope that this fosters other conversations with people of different identities, cultures, and religions.

Chapter 5, "Galatians 2:11–14: An Ideological Strategy," is the strategy that best reflects my position. This strategy brings identity to bear on interpretation as well, but in a less particular way than the dialogical approach (ch. 4) and in a more general or communal way (ch. 3), drawing on what we all have in common: recognition and hospitality. Thus in examining a particular text, Gal 2:11–14, centered on the theme of recognition (identity—Paul and Cephas) and hospitality (how we receive difference), I proceed by discussing the understanding of this theme in the present and then apply this understanding to the text itself, allowing space for the text itself to speak through a constructed close reading of the text. Similar to the dialogical approach, this chapter also aims to spark a conversation between readers about sameness and difference (recognition) and how we receive difference and how difference integrates into sameness (hospitality).

The final chapter, "Latino/a Biblical Interpretation: Is It a Question of Being and/or Practice?," brings an ongoing question back to the forefront. I address the question briefly in the second chapter, but here I develop it a bit more. This question draws attention to the sociopolitical conditions that enabled the development of what has come to be known as Latino/a biblical interpretation. What initiates such a discussion is whether

---

31. Grant with Tracy, *Short History*, 170.

Latino/a identity takes precedence over anyone (i.e., non-Latino/a) practicing Latino/a biblical interpretation. By asking this question, Latinos/
as, for example, signal a distrust or a concern that non-Latinos/as might
claim as much socially, if not more (if they spoke Spanish or worked with
Latinos/as), in common with the experience of Latinos/as than with other
non-Latinos/as.[32] This is a very important and serious question, but it
assumes an essentializing of Latino/a identity that does not take into the
account the multiple identifications that are in existence today, such as
ethnic/racial mixed identities and Latinx identities. Latino/a biblical interpretation as a project might better serve itself by moving away from the
question of identity and closer to intersectionality, where the crisscrossing
of identities is in play. In this way, broadening the concept of identity leads
to a greater level of recognition, perhaps, and a wider audience.

Together the core chapters (3–5) highlight the heart of the hermeneutic experience, namely, application.[33] As I often mention to students,
reading about Latino/a biblical interpretation, as well as other interpretations, is a good way to start a conversation with yourself and others on how
you yourself would construct an interpretive strategy. In this way, reading
texts (ancient and modern) becomes more meaningful to you. At a time
when representing difference (i.e., a Latino/a identity) and different ways
of being (ontology) and knowing (epistemology) are coming under attack
as belonging to specific groups or as purely biased in their interpretations,
the task of understanding as many types of cultural biblical interpretations as possible is important.[34] This is not to say that Latino/a biblical

---

32. A similar concern is expressed by Latina feminists about white feminists,
with the latter assuming they have much in common with Latina feminists doing
Latina interpretation because they share the experience of patriarchy. These analo-
gies can be extended to queer readers vis-à-vis straight readers, African American
women vis-à-vis white women, white readers vis-à-vis Native American readers, white Asian studies scholars vis-à-vis Asian scholars, or able-bodied readers
vis-à-vis disabled-bodied readers. This concern has much merit, but a factor to
consider is context. For instance, if a publisher is putting together a Latino/a commentary series and invites an Anglo to write on Luke, for example, but there are
plenty of Latino/a Lukan scholars to pick from, this would draw concern. But if
there are no Latino/a Lukan scholars whatsoever, the publisher has no choice but
to select someone from outside the community.

33. See Palmer, *Hermeneutics*, 186–91.

34. Here I am thinking of the vitriolic political rhetoric in the United States

interpretation is without its limitations, but listening to the demands of the present as well as the voice of the text can bring about transformation and liberation to all God's people in the present.

(2016–2017) against newly arrived migrants and against the integrity of judges (e.g., US District Judge Gonzalo P. Curiel) in their consideration of arguments.

2

Toward Latino/a Biblical Studies: Foregrounding Identities and Transforming Communities

What does it mean to do Latino/a biblical studies or hermeneutics? In this chapter, I shall attempt to address this question not by examining a history of scholarship in the field but by critically examining the meaning and implication of the three designations in question—Latino/a, biblical, and studies. It is not my intention here to merely define these terms. Rather, this is meant to be a discussion about how these three interlocking components interact to form the basis for how I see myself doing Latino/a biblical studies. As I am influenced by reading all sorts of hermeneutical approaches, from early tradition to the present,[1] the hope is that this work will also participate in the history of interpretation, thus conveying a sense of belongingness but being apart (having a unique identity). The intent is that the chapter will inspire others to construct and reflect on their own hermeneutics.

This is a revised and updated version of an essay originally published as "Toward Latino/a Biblical Studies: Foregrounding Identities and Transforming Communities," in *Latino/a Biblical Hermeneutics: Problematics, Objectives, Strategies*, ed. Francisco Lozada Jr. and Fernando F. Segovia, SemeiaSt 68 (Atlanta: SBL Press, 2014), 187–202.

1. See Henning Graf Reventlow, *History of Biblical Interpretation*, trans. Leo G. Purdue and Jim Duke, 4 vols., RBS 50, 61–63 (Atlanta: Society of Biblical Literature, 2009–2010). These four volumes are the finest and most comprehensive work on the historical influences and participants in the history of interpretation, from the Hebrew Bible to the twentieth century. The end of the history is lacking a bit, ending with Rudolf Bultmann and excluding women, for example, from the history, which speaks to the "patriarchalization" of the field.

Latino/a biblical studies and hermeneutics, like many other approaches based on ideological and/or contextual frameworks, are not uniform or universal in strategy or orientation. They are quite diverse and particular in approaches, aims, and principles. For instance, two principles that underlie my own particular understanding of Latino/a biblical studies are (1) the foregrounding of Latino/a identities and (2) the transformation of the Latino/a community from one of marginality in the political sphere to a community that has gained some representation or belongingness in various mainstream institutions, including religious communities. These principles are expressed in the interpretative processes of engaging the text and evaluating those Latino/a readings of the text that are employed in the field.

The first principle concerns the foregrounding of Latino/a identity or identities. This foregrounding may be expressed in various ways, but the underlying principle focuses on the dynamic relationship between the reader's personal and communal identity(ies), the community's or communities' histories, the sources emanating from the community, and other social factors that combine to help the reader engage the text from a Latino/a context. In this way, the Latino/a identity(ies), contexts, and conditions become prime factors in what it means to do Latino/a biblical studies.

The second principle involves the transformation of the Latino/a community from a marginal social group to one that has achieved significant representation and belongingness in the religious, social, and political systems. This does not mean that the Latino/a community has been assimilated into these systems, nor does it mean that the community has simply become distinct from other communities in these systems. Rather, this principle suggests that Latino/a biblical studies and hermeneutics must contribute in some way toward assisting Latinos/as and others to gain access to a variety of systems and aim to establish significant representation and belongingness in these systems. This transformation affects not only the Latino/a community, but other ethnic/racial groups as well.

Now that I have identified the principles that underlie my approach to this work, the remainder of this chapter consists of three main sections. The first section examines the expression *Latino/a* by exploring the complexity behind the nomenclature and issues regarding who can do Latino/a biblical studies and hermeneutics. The second section examines the expression *biblical* by exploring what it signifies and what a Latino/a approach to the text looks like. Finally, the third section examines the term *studies* by exploring what it suggests within the field of Latino/a studies. I hope, via this examination, not only to present my framework for doing the work of Latino/a biblical studies and hermeneutics but also, and perhaps more importantly, to begin a discussion of the field in general and of the essential questions of Latinos/as in particular. My goal is not to provide a definitive answer regarding Latino/a biblical studies and hermeneutics but to give readers some tools to evaluate the field and perhaps scaffolding for proposing or developing a perspective of their own.

Latino/a as Concept

The concept (or adjective) *Latino/a* is an issue of contention inside and outside the Latino/a communities.[2] What does the term signify? Is it an expression that points to ethnic/racial formations of one or both parents, gender and sexuality formations combined with ethnic/racial formations,[3] and/or national and/or geographical formations of a group of people in the United States whose ancestry is most recently traced back to Latin America (including the Caribbean) or the US Southwest? Is it a term that points to racial hereditary background in Spain, Africa, and/or indigenous communities spread throughout the Americas? Is it a term that captures the identity of people whose native tongue was once or still is Spanish or one of the many indigenous dialects? Or does it signify a group with a

---

2. Three concise introductions to the history and identity of Latinos/as in the United States are: Juan Gonzalez, *Harvest of Empire: A History of Latinos in America*, rev. ed. (New York: Penguin, 2011); David G. Gutiérrez, ed., *The Columbia History of Latinos in the United States since 1960* (New York: Columbia University Press, 2004); Ruth Enid Zambrana, *Latinos in American Society: Families and Communities in Transition* (Ithaca, NY: Cornell University Press, 2011). All three volumes informed much of my narrative on the cultural history of Latinos/as in this chapter and throughout the volume.

3. See the following volumes on Latino/a identity and sexuality formations, including questions of immigration: Eithne Luibhéid and Lionel Cantú Jr., eds., *Queer Migrations: Sexuality, U.S. Citizenship, and Border Crossings* (Minneapolis: University of Minnesota Press, 2005); Cantú, *The Sexuality of Migration: Border Crossings and Mexican Immigrant Men*, ed. Nancy A. Naples and Salvador Vidal Ortiz, Intersections: Transdisciplinary Perspectives on Genders and Sexualities (New York: New York University Press, 2009).

shared history of colonialism at the hands of Spain, Roman Catholicism, and Protestantism?

The term Latino/a is simply a slippery term with no hard boundaries to define it. The task of delineating it is very challenging, as it means different things to different peoples and groups. For instance, not all Latinos/as point to a national identity in the traditional sense (e.g., Chicanos). Nor do all Latinos/as share the same ethnic/racial background (e.g., black Latino/a/x, indigenous Latino/a/x, white Latino/a/x) or religious identity (e.g., Christian, Muslim, Jewish) or philosophical orientation (e.g., humanist, agnostic, atheist). Nor do all Latinos/as speak Spanish or see their identity anchored in a paradigm of pan-nationalism. However, what many Latino/a groups do seem to have in common is the perception by non-Latino/a that they are Others in the United States—simply here visiting. Even so, conceptually, the term Latino/a remains difficult to fix, as it is constantly changing based on the cultural and political landscape of those who identify as Hispanic, Latino, Latina, or Latino/a in the United States. The term is either well received, rejected, or, at times, used interchangeably with other comparable terms, signaling other significations. Thus the term Latino/a remains fluid within the Latino/a communities throughout the United States, although some scholars are keen to fix the identity along hereditary lines (or via what is termed *essentialism*). One avenue we may use to begin to grasp the background or signification of the term Latino/a is to explore the various Latino/a groups' collective histories in the United States and their engagement with the larger political society.

Another way of identifying this collective, although it is not as ubiquitous as it once was, is the term *Hispanics* or *Hispanic Americans*. This term no longer frequently used because its history is quite conflicted. For some this term identifies Spain rather than Latin America as their most recent ancestral home. For these individuals, Hispanic accurately speaks to their experience in the United States. For others, the term is anathema and signifies internalized colonialism, particularly because the United States government employed it for the purposes of the US Census in 1980.[4]

---

4. For a brief discussion on the use of the term *Hispanic* and its first appearance on the 1980 census form, see Clara Rodríguez, *Changing Race: Latinos, the Census, and the History of Ethnicity in the United States*, Critical America (New York: New York University Press, 2000), 159–63.

Conversely, the term Latino/a is perceived by some people as an emic designation—one that emanates from within the group—that contains political
significance and agency. For these individuals, the term Hispanic not only
signifies the relationship to Spain but also evokes the notions of assimilation, neutrality, and group invisibility in the political arena. However, an
either/or construct attached to either of these terms seems flawed, as many
people (not all) use both terms interchangeably and with different intents.

Historically, the terms *Latinos/as* (*Latino/a*) and *Hispanic* were not
viable designations used within the groups under discussion. Instead,
members of differing Latino/a groups identified themselves via their
geographical and national origin (e.g., Cubano/a, Puertorriqueño/a,
Mexicano/a, Dominicano/a, Colombiano/a). The tradition of using one's
ethnic particularities to identify subgroup membership generally remained
private, while in the public arena one of the nomenclatures referring to the
broader collective, Latino/a or Hispanic, was more commonly used. One
major exception to this rule is that specific subgroups can create their own
labels for political and/or economic purposes.

For instance, in the 1960s, to reflect their unity during the labor
and political battles that took place in the Southwest and West (e.g., the
United Farm Workers under César Chávez and Dolores Huerta, *Raza
Unida* in Texas), many Mexican Americans referred to themselves as
Chicanos/as, a term that they still use today, particularly within certain
institutional and regional contexts, to signify their continued unity. This
inclination to nationalize identity based on a paradigm of race and/or
ethnicity is also reflected among the population of Puerto Ricans living
in New York. These Latinos/as identify themselves as Nuyoricans, a
designation that is partially the result of battles for equal rights waged
by the New York chapter of the Young Lords political party. Similarly,
after their migration to the United States as political refugees and exiles
beginning in the 1960s, many Cubans began to nationalize their identity
by using a hyphen, Cuban-Americans, as a way to politically and eco-
nomically position themselves as a minoritized or ethnic/racial group
among Latinos/as or Hispanics in the United States. These names are
also commonly used among Latino/a intellectuals and activists, including many (but not all) Latino/a biblical interpreters, theologians, and
religion scholars, who are influenced by or engage in Latino/a cultural
studies. In the years to come, it will be interesting to discover how and
if cultural national identity is reflected among the newer or more recent

Latin American migrant[5] communities. It will also be quite interesting to see if these nation-based understandings of ethnicity/race filter into Latino/a biblical studies and hermeneutics.

However, even though there continues to be political, economic, and social challenges within ethnic/racial subgroups, this naming history (i.e., Latino/a or Hispanic) does not always continue with second- and third-generation Latinos/as, who may no longer look toward or dream of their parents' or grandparents' homeland or identity but instead resonate more with the experiences of other Latinos/as in the United States. This seems especially pertinent for those who are living or teaching in multiple Latino/a ethnic/racial communities and who see the United States as home. For these individuals, the notion of the collective Other outweighs the notion of national or geographical identities. This image of Latino/a as Other is portrayed across modes of discourse, including film, literature, and television profiles, as well as scriptural, theological, sermonic, and political discourses. Interestingly, this Othering, especially when it involves antimigrant or nativist discourses, reconnects second- and third-generation Latinos/as with their parents' or ancestors' migrant past or colonial history, such as Mexican Americans in the Southwest or Dominicans in the Northeast. Indeed, the incorporation of this Othering has served to consolidate and perhaps solidify the racial/ethnic consciousness and organization of Latinos/as in the current era.

What does this all have to do with biblical studies? Simply put, the constantly changing complex web of social, historical, and political factors involved in the construction of Latino/a identity is the basis of a Latino/a reading of the biblical text. In other words, each reader/interpreter brings his or her (their) own unique identity set to the text, and this provides the worldview through which the meaning and the relevance of the narrative is determined. This is an essential component of the approach. The

---

5. In this chapter and throughout the volume, I am following the lead of Eithne Luibhéid, who employs the term *migrant* to refer to all those who cross international borders (land, air, or sea), whether legally or undocumented. The word can refer to documented or undocumented immigrants, refugees, asylum seekers, or, even colonial subjects remade as commonwealth citizens. As she indicates, these descriptors are constantly changing, depending on the status of migrants. See Luibhéid, "Introduction: Queering Migration and Citizenship," in Luibhéid and Cantú, *Queer Migrations*, xi.

foregrounding of Latino/a identity, specifically, is what differentiates this approach from, say, Latin American, African American, Asian American, Native American, or other contextual readings that are based on very different political and historical realities.[6] Of course, it is also very dissimilar from those readings of the text that do not consider identity at all as well as those that claim to be solely informed by the principle of objectivity during the reading experience.

The inclusion of the reader's identity into the dynamics of interpretation allows not only for the particularity of each Latino/a ethnic/racial group to emerge but also for the particularity of each reader within these groups, with the aim of providing new insights in their respective readings. In this way, it destabilizes any potential master narrative that might mistakenly assume that a Puerto Rican, Mexican American, Cuban American, Dominican American, Salvadoran American, Guatemalan American, or Bolivian American (to name a few) reading is representative of the views of the entire Latino/a community in the United States. It also negates the idea that ethnic identity and race are the only modalities that define Latino/a. Indeed, there are other, competing modalities at work, such as class, gender, sexual orientation, and religious or political affiliation, that also speak to the particularity of the reader or community. Most importantly, by foregrounding the Latino/a experience, this approach destabilizes not only the myth that the United States is a homogeneous, monolingual, or monocultural country, but it also destabilizes the script that the field of biblical studies is done the same way by everyone and that its practitioners are identical. Said another way, it challenges the notion that the production of knowledge emanates from one particular, exclusive economic and socioeducational community.

As noted, the inclusion of Latino/a identity in the reading experience of texts may also touch upon many issues affecting Latinos/as, such as colonial and neocolonial realities and the current cultural representations of Latinos/as. For instance, at the colonial level, this approach engages the factors that bring Latinos/as together—such as their colonial histories (1492–1898)—by examining the implementation of imperial political, religious, and economic policies. Such policies have led to the subjugation of

---

6. For an understanding of some of the similarities in reading strategies among minoritized biblical studies, see Segovia, "Poetics of Minority Biblical Criticism," 279–311.

indigenous peoples; the homogenization of communities; the exploitation of the working class; the colonial acquisition of land; the dislocation of many Latinos/as in the United States; and the colonial cultural, political, and religious ideologies implemented by Christian theology in particular (e.g., Manifest Destiny and the Monroe Doctrine). At the neocolonial level (1898–present), the approach focuses on the influences of Latino/a particularity and collective identity. This includes topics such as immigration laws, guest-worker programs, and economic and foreign policies, all of which are part of what it means to be Latino/a in the United States. At the cultural level (past and present), foregrounding the Latino/a experience allows one to be aware of how it is constructed through the Internet, television, print media, and other forms of global and geopolitical communication. It is at this level that a closer examination of the foregrounding of the Latino/a identity presents the most challenging—but necessary—course of study, since it must also include the issues of Black Latinos/as and people of mixed Latino/a backgrounds as well as issues such as masculinity, sexism, language, education, class, and religion. In sum, the construct of *Latino/a* is a nomenclature that strongly defines what it means to do Latino/a biblical studies, yet it is always between some notion of fixity and fluidity and so must be located and studied both historically and politically.

A final question needs to be briefly considered here. The volume will take it up again in the conclusion. Does someone need to be Latino/a to do Latino/a biblical studies? That is, can someone be, say, Anglo-American, African American, or Asian American and still do Latino/a biblical studies? The answer to this question depends on whether one sees *Latino/a* from an essentialist-leaning or a constructionist-leaning point of view. In other words, does one need to be descended from or biologically related to someone who is Latino/a (an essentialist perspective), or can someone who is not Latino/a but is committed to Latino/a issues of social justice and a liberating representation also be a legitimate practitioner of Latino/a biblical studies (a constructionist perspective)? Some Latino/a critics would argue that it is desirable to have a combination of the two perspectives, thus moving the question away from an either/or toward a both/and scenario.

One might ask whether such a question is even relevant. The question is important, because there is concern among essentialists that non-Latinos/as will use the growing popularity of the field (and population) to attempt to speak for a community that they may only understand from an etic

perspective. Thus, essentialists feel that there is a hazard that these scholars may misrepresent the experience of the broader Latino/a community.
This was and continues to be an issue with other contextual hermeneutic
communities as well—namely, who can speak for the "subaltern"? Another
related issue is that non-Latino/a scholars often do not have a direct invest-
ment in the community, and so they are presumably not subject to the
same dynamics and conditions as *actual* community members. Because of
this, essentialists contend that it is best that people who do not have ethnic
ties to the community not practice Latino/a biblical studies.

Conversely, those who lean toward the constructionist perspective
that one does not have to be Latino/a to do Latino/a biblical studies believe
that the Latino/a community needs all the allies it can muster to contribute to and provide a positive representation of the Latino/a community.
From this latter perspective, all practitioners who are sincere in the work
are welcome. I position myself and my work closer to the constructionist
position, but cautiously so. This is because what is of greatest significance
to me is that the Latino/a experience and dynamic should be at the core
of the work and that the work should provide a positive representation of
Latino/a identity and the Latino/a community.[7] I believe that these elements are crucial to the field, regardless of the scholar's background. Still, I
remain conflicted because foregrounding and the challenge of representation, even when one is doing it with the best intentions, can be problematic.
For instance, a Latino/a scholar can foreground Latino/a identity in a
universal, objective, and positivistic fashion or construct a Latino/a representational identity in a very myopic or stereotypical fashion. For this
reason, all Latino/a readings of the text must undergo a critique.

In sum, the question of whether to use an essentialist perspective, a
constructionist perspective, or both remains a key issue in the field, one
strongly debated. These types of questions—who is a Latino/a, what constitutes Latino/a identity, and what constitutes Latino/a biblical studies and
hermeneutics in general—are ongoing in the field. This tension between
fixing Latino/a identity (essentialist) and seeing Latino/a identity as fluid
(constructionist) demonstrate that the field is still emerging and that

---

7. I say "cautiously so" because the context of a situation is also a variable to
consider. See n. 32 in chapter 1.

understanding its contours and shape is a task that will continue for the foreseeable future.

Biblical as Concept

The second concept under discussion is *biblical*. Unlike the term Latino/a, the concept biblical is not as ambiguous within the field. Here it refers to the canonical writings of the Bible. For the majority of Latino/a scholars in the field, the object of examination is the Christian Bible, that is, the Hebrew Bible and New Testament. Unlike Latino/a scholars in other fields, who may focus primarily on the question of identity within their respective disciplines (e.g., ethnography, history, literature), in this field, the Christian Bible and its reception have been and remain the focus of study. In addition, to my knowledge, research has also focused strictly on the "canonical" texts that play a major role in the faith of the Latino/a community.

The Latino/a interpreter's stance toward the process of interpreting biblical texts varies. Most interpreters work under the assumption that the text is sacred. However, this does not preclude the interpreter from engaging the text critically or from challenging the idea that the word of God is synonymous with the words of the text. Nor does it, for the most part, inhibit the interpreter's understanding of the world/context behind the text. Indeed, for many Latino/a interpreters, the text is examined (or read) in a way that includes the condition of the interpreter or his/her community, thus reifying the notion that the text is speaking to the conditions of the community. Much of this theological assumption is strongly influenced by liberation hermeneutics, which, generally speaking, holds that God is on the side of the oppressed/marginalized and that this support is made visible (revealed) through the stories of marginalization and liberation in the biblical text. This stance toward the text is, therefore, one in which the word of God is present in the text as well as in the interpreter's/community's respective experience. The text is therefore sacred in making sense of their reality and marginality.

Much of this theological assumption is also supported by strategies that correlate the experience of the interpreter/community with the experience of those marginalized in the stories. It is this theological aspect that is accentuated in the process of interpretation rather than in the context of the text. In other words, the experience of marginality in the text is analogous to the experience of the interpreter and his or her (their) community in the present. Certain methodological approaches are used to support this strategy, such as historical criticism or the social- or literary-critical approaches. It is interesting to note that, at moments, the critical social and literary approaches may also be seen as allegorical approaches to reading. Thus interpretations using these approaches are presented without any engagement or assessment of how the approach is used or applied. Unfortunately, this lack of examination may in turn lead to the mistaken assumption that one's interpretation is liberative for the community and others who are marginalized.

Other Latino/a interpreters have created a different framework for understanding the sacredness of the text. For these scholars, the text is considered sacred in the sense that it plays a vital role in the construc- tion of Christian identity within the Christian tradition and therefore is a living and lived text. However, from this perspective the text undergoes an examination of its context relative to its production and reception. In addition, the interpreter is also contextualized, usually by way of fore- grounding his or her (their) identity. Given that the text is viewed as an active participant in the construction and representation of a mar- ginal identity, it is approached pointedly and suspiciously and thus must undergo an examination that allows for its ideological dimensions to be scrutinized. Methods such as minoritized biblical approaches, ideological criticism in its many forms, feminist criticism, or imperial studies allow for this perspective, which also identifies the text as sacred not in the sense that the reality of the world behind the text corresponds to the reality of Latinos/as but rather in the sense that it participates in the construction and representation of Latino/a Christian identity as well as the identity of others. Still, these types of construction must be evaluated for their rami- fications for the community and toward other minoritized communities.

This focus on the Christian Bible leads to different engagements with the text framed around different reading strategies. The two framings that I discuss and which I alluded to above are examples of the use of cor- relation and ideological readings as ways to engage the text. The former correlates the stories of marginality with the changing historical or social conditions of the reader and his or her (their) community, while the latter confronts any ideological conceptions or perceived worldview of the text that may shed light on the human condition in general or the Latino/a identity in particular. Another strategy engages the text as a dialogue partner, thus using the reading experience as a launching pad to explore other issues within the text and/or within the Latino/a community. The goal is to glean new insights into certain issues and themes from the text that are based on the reader's identity. The next part of this discussion examines these three reading strategies, beginning with the one that I perceive best represents how a majority engages Latino/a biblical studies.

The Text as Correlation

This particular tactic correlates the historical experience of marginality of the characters (historical figures for many) in the narratives of the text with similar and concurrent experiences of marginality among Latinos/as.[8] The biblical text, therefore, is seen as a mirror of sorts between the world behind the text and the world in front of the text (i.e., the world of the reader). Thus, the text is an avenue that joins the current Latino/a experience and reality to the reality within the biblical text. In other words, the biblical text is engaged from a Latino/a perspective with the hope of an encounter that relates to or is analogous to the Latino/a experience. Sometimes this process takes the form of a strong dichotomy between context and text, where the context of the reader is first presented ("My social location is …"), followed by an analysis of the text, so that the former will make a contribution toward understanding the latter. At other times, this process takes the form of a cross-textual experience, where the reader's Latino/a identity and the narrative are both seen as texts and examined accordingly. The Latino/a reader, therefore, works under the assumption that his or her (their) context contributes to the interpretation of the text.

---

8. For a recent volume that demonstrates elements of this strategy, see M. Daniel Carroll R., *Christians at the Border: Immigration, the Church, and the Bible* (Grand Rapids: Baker Academic, 2008). Others studies in the history of scholarship in Latino/a biblical interpretation that employ a text-as-correlation strategy, though not exclusively, include David Cortés-Fuentes, "Not Like the Gentiles: The Characterization of Gentiles in the Gospel according to St. Matthew," in *JHLT* 9 (2001): 6–26; Pablo Jiménez, "The Bible: A Hispanic Perspective," in *Teologia en conjunto: A Collaborative Hispanic Protestant Theology*, ed. José David Rodriguez and Loida I. Martell-Otero (Louisville: Westminster John Knox, 1997), 66–79; Romero, *Hispanic Devotional Piety*.

The reader also understands oneself as a Latino/a biblical scholar as well as a Latino/a Christian theologian. The biblical text, therefore, is viewed most often as an ally in the quest for a transformative experience of some nature within the Latino/a community. Correlating the experiences of Latinos/as as members of a marginal group (ethnic/racial marginality, that is) with the experience of those marginalized in the text calls on readers to resonate with the biblical story even more. The theological assumption is that this resonance indicates that God is on the side of Latinos/as.

The Text as Dialogical Partner

This particular tactic involves using the text as a way to speak about a particular issue that pertains primarily to the identity of the interpreter as well as to the issues of a text.[9] In other words, the text is used as a sounding board to explore issues that pertain to the realities of the Latino/a interpreter and how these realities open the door to exploring the identity of a text. Current issues such as immigration, language, and hybridity, for example, are used to explore migration, language, and hybridity in the biblical text. The methodological approaches employed may vary, but literary approaches are the most widely used. The text as a dialogical partner is in many ways also a conversation partner. There is very little confrontation of the text. Instead,

---

9. For an illustrative essay that draws from this reading strategy, see Francisco García-Treto, "Exile in the Hebrew Bible: A Postcolonial Look from the Cuban Diaspora," in Bailey, Liew, and Segovia, *They Were All Together*, 65–78. Other studies that make use of this text-as-dialogical-partner strategy, though not exclusively, include Efraín Agosto, "Paul vs. Empire: A Postcolonial and Latino Reading," *Perspectivas: Occasional Papers* 6 (2002): 37–56; Agosto, "The Letter to the Philippians," in *A Postcolonial Commentary on the New Testament Writings*, ed. Fernando F. Segovia and R. S. Sugirtharajah, Bible and Postcolonialism 13 (London: T&T Clark, 2007), 281–93; Osvaldo D. Vena, "My Hermeneutical Journey and Daily Journey into Hermeneutics: Meaning-Making and Biblical Interpretation in the North American Diaspora," in *Interpreting beyond Borders*, ed. Fernando F. Segovia, Bible and Postcolonialism 3 (Sheffield: Sheffield Academic, 2000), 84–106; Leticia A. Guardiola-Sáenz, "Border-Crossing and Its Redemptive Power in John 7:53–8:11: A Cultural Reading of Jesus and the *Accused*," in *John and Postcolonialism: Travel, Space and Power*, ed. Musa W. Dube and Jeffrey L. Staley, Bible and Postcolonialism 7 (Sheffield: Sheffield Academic, 2002), 129–52.

many scholars employ the text to agree, disagree, or problematize an issue in the narrative or in the general experience of Latinos/as. Since the process of interpretation involves the construction of the Latino/a Christian identity, the text is engaged in a way that makes sense of or produces an image of an identity that assists in this particular construction.

The Text as Ideology

This particular tactic involves employing the text as a point of departure to explore issues related to Latino/a identity.[10] In other words, it is not just the text that undergoes explorative analysis of its composition but also aspects of the reader and his or her (their) community. Therefore, personal factors such as gender, ethnicity, race, and language become the focus of analysis as well. This look at the text as ideology involves employing a dialogue within Latino/a studies to expose any issues, silences, or absences reflected in the history of engagement with the text. In other words, the biblical text is explored to foster both a better understanding of the text itself and, more importantly, a better understanding of the particular aspect of the reader (or his or her [their] community) that the reader wishes to discuss. The overall aim is that engaging the text with different tactics will bring a new point of view to the text. It functions to make other readers see differently how the text might be reinterpreted.

The biblical text, therefore, is viewed as an ideological discourse partner for a transformative experience that helps other readers understand the identity formations that emerge within the Latino/a community, which perhaps may not be so obvious. As such, for some Latino/a critics of the biblical text, the text is seen as ideological. Whereas the first strategy (correlation approach) mentioned above might be framed as "speaking complicatedly

---

10. For a recent representative volume that draws from this strategy, see Ruiz, *Readings from the Edges*. Other interpretations that utilize a text-as-ideological strategy, though not necessarily exclusively, include Robert D. Maldonado, "¿La Conquista? Latin American (*Mestizaje*) Reflections on the Biblical Conquest," *JHLT* 2 (1995): 5–25; "Reading Malinche Reading Ruth: Toward a Hermeneutics of Betrayal," *Semeia* 72 (1995): 91–110; Fernando F. Segovia, "Inclusion and Exclusion in John 17: An Intercultural Reading," in *Literary and Social Readings of the Fourth Gospel*, vol. 2 of *"What Is John?,"* ed. Fernando F. Segovia, SymS 3 (Atlanta: Scholars Press, 1998), 183–210.

with" the biblical text, and the second strategy (dialogical approach) might be seen as "speaking interactively with" the biblical text, the third strategy (ideological approach) is viewed along the lines of "speaking back to" the text. The text is an Other; yet it also participates, although not exclusively, in constructing the Other as marginal through its history of interpretations. The text is viewed as a medium to be examined in various ways with the intent to understand the power dynamics at play in the narratives. In turn, such analyses are used to help Latino/a scholars of the Bible better understand the power or political dynamics in the world of Latinos/as.

As already alluded to, these three approaches do not have clear boundaries. Each blends into the other; yet for this study's purposes, they are demarcations that provide heuristic understandings of how some Latinos/as engage the biblical text. The different strategies or tactics of Latino/a biblical studies continue to include more varied points of reference to inform its readings, including cultural and environmental studies. Even the expansion of questions like "What is biblical?" to questions like "What is Scripture?" expands the discussion to include other religious texts and readings from a Latino/a perspective. In the subsequent three chapters, I employ each one of these reading strategies (text as correlation, text as dialogical partner, and text as ideology) as illustrative examples of various modes of Latino/a biblical hermeneutics.

Studies as Concept

The third concept that we will examine here is *studies*. What does this term signify in the context of Latino/a biblical studies? To answer this question, I will engage in an analysis of the four dominant paradigms of biblical criticism. Specifically, the remainder of this discussion will address historical criticism, cultural criticism, literary criticism, and ideological criticism and how each is involved in or related to Latino/a biblical studies.

Historical Criticism

There is no question that historical criticism still has a strong foothold in the field of biblical interpretation. Its presuppositions are that meaning exists in the world behind the text as something to be extracted or excavated and that the interpreter of the text is a neutral party, who, at his or her (their) best, is able to maintain objectivity, promote positivism, and support universality. For Latino/a biblical studies specifically, historical criticism still plays a major role. Its role may not be direct; yet it continues to inform the work of many scholars—even though the principles and assumptions that uphold the paradigm are challenged at times. This means that no longer are the principles of objectivity, positivism, or universality believed to be inherent in historical reconstructions of the text. Instead, scholars have become aware that, although some historical distance from the text is desirable, the assumption that using the historical-critical method implies complete objectivity is no longer viable. In other words, no perspective or interpretation is completed in a vacuum. Given this, some scholars wonder whether the approach—developed during the age of European Enlightenment—remains relevant or useful as a tool for Latino/a biblical studies. Many also wonder if the field of Latino/a biblical studies requires specific analytical tools that are developed exclusively for and within the Latino/a experience. These issues remain points of debate in the field.

Cultural Criticism

Similar to historical criticism, certain tools from this particular paradigm are employed in Latino/a biblical studies. The text is viewed as a means to discerning both the social world of the text and the social codes/language within the text. Although the underlying principles of this approach are similar to those of the historical approach, there is a difference in their use and application in Latino/a biblical studies. The body of literature based on this perspective is still small, but it continues to play a minor role in the reading strategies of some Latino/a biblical interpreters. I suspect the issues of poverty, class, and family that shape the discourse of Latinos/as in the present will give way to a fuller employment of this approach in the near future—including broadening the contours to include discussions of sexuality, economics, and geopolitics within and in front of the text.

Literary Criticism

Again, similar to historical criticism, the tools from this paradigm are used frequently in Latino/a biblical studies. From this perspective, the text is viewed as a medium between the reader and the narrative of the text. I would argue that the principles of neutrality, objectivity, positivism, and universality are more prevalent in literary criticism than they are in historical criticism, particularly in the text-dominant approaches of literary criticism (e.g., narrative criticism). This is less so in the reader-dominant approaches (e.g., reader-response readings). Interestingly, it is this latter, reader-dominant approach that opened a door for Latinos/as to explore how their social location influenced the story world of the biblical text. Like the historical approach, literary criticism continues to be used as a tool, among many others, that provides understanding of the narrative text for the Latino/a community. However, literary criticism is simply a tool that allows us to see not just the narrative as text but also the engaged reader or community as a text that also must be scrutinized.

Ideological Criticism

The last paradigm that I wish to discuss is ideological criticism. Moving away from the assumptions of neutrality, objectivity, positivism, and universality found in historical criticism and literary criticism, ideological criticism is an approach that not only engages the text as a historical or rhetorical document but also identifies the text as an ideological document. From this perspective, the text is a repository of information, but it is always positioned or constructed information and always influenced by the role of the interpreter and his or her positionality. Ideological criticism provides a wider platform from which one can engage both the biblical text and the reader's Latino/a identity as constructions. In this way it provides an avenue for Latino/a biblical criticism to explore other tools and strategies for interpreting text, such as "reading with" or "reading against" the ideological worldview of the text.

Ideological criticism also embraces postcolonial approaches. It is the foregrounding of the legacy of colonial, neocolonial, and postcolonial history that informs my engagement of the question of Latino/a identity as well as the biblical tradition. Regarding Latino/a identity, the approach focuses on understanding how US and European scholarship (from European colonial countries) have constructed Latino/a identity and its particularities. It notes that scholars based in the United States and Europe have codified this identity as Other and examines how this process of Othering occurred, particularly through the history of colonization. This method also applies to Roman Catholicism and Protestantism, since these religious bodies have contributed to the social construction of Latinos/

as as the Other through religious instruction, missionary endeavors, and other colonial activities. In addition, the approach examines the resistant writing of Latinos/as as a way to undo the colonizing characterization and "natural" constructions of Latinos/as as colonial subjects. It aims to highlight the value of Latino/a identity and identify Latinos/as as moral agents. With regard to biblical tradition, the postcolonial approach is applied to how US and European scholars have constructed a colonial framework of the world behind, in, and in front of the text, through which they study the biblical tradition. At the same time, the postcolonial approach provides alternative readings of the text and reclaims the text's meaning for those affected by colonization and oppression in today's world.

Finally, I see ideological criticism as providing an opening for liberation hermeneutics to enter the discourse. I feel that liberation hermeneutics is the other area that identifies me as a Latino/a biblical critic. For me, this approach, like postcolonial studies or Latino/a cultural studies, is not a method per se but rather an ideological orientation toward the text and the reader or the reading communities. My position of liberation is not simply focused on the economic factors of Latin America. It also intersects with the hope that all marginalized peoples will be liberated from oppression. Liberation hermeneutics—as I see it—does not aim to reassert the authority of the text or the authority of the reader but rather aims to engage both, with the goal of sifting out what is liberative and what is not from such interaction with or readings of texts. Most importantly, it always provides the space for such readings to be challenged by others. Like postcolonialism, my use of liberation hermeneutics allows me to interpret the reading process as resistance reading and the text as problematic in the sense that it is not the only source for morality and theology—context plays a role in the decision-making process.I engage or employ liberation hermeneutics not as a way to search for liberation in the biblical text but rather as an ethos, along with Latino/a studies and ideological studies.

Conclusion

In this chapter I have sought to provide a general understanding of what Latino/a biblical studies is all about. By exploring the separate but intertwined concepts of *Latino/a*, *biblical*, and *studies*, I have attempted to discuss some of the issues, objectives, and problems involved with the field while simultaneously presenting my framework for engagement in discussing the field and the principles and assumptions I currently employ in applying the approach. To conclude, for myself, both the foregrounding of Latino/a identity and the transformation of the Latino/a community are principles that shape my work within the discourse of Latino/a biblical studies. In what follows, I shall provide sample interpretative readings of various texts emanating from each of the three different readings strategies mentioned above. It is important to keep in mind once again that the three illustrative readings presented in the following chapters are not a typology, nor are they exhaustive. They are simply a series of readings illustrating the diverse ways in which Latino/a biblical interpretation can be construed.

3

Journey and the Fourth Gospel: A Correlation Strategy

As mentioned in the first chapter, what follows is an example of reading along the lines of correlation. Such an approach is not universal among Latino/a scholars, but it is present in many analyses, especially in the early stages of Latino/a biblical hermeneutics and among Latino/a theologians employing the Bible. The aim is to correlate the social location of the interpreter or community with the narrative story or issue in the text. In other words, the text is reproduced in the context of the interpreter or community by way of the plot, character, or marginalization of a community. A guiding principle of such a strategy, as I see it, is one that sees the text as addressing modern issues, with an assumption that the representation of the story world, whatever that might be, can be correlated to the context of the interpreter or that the representation of the story world, whatever that might be, awakens the interpreter to the realities of his or her (their) context.[1] This chapter will attempt to do the same by correlating the theme of journey found in the Fourth Gospel with the theme of Latino/a migration that is so present in the reality and/or memory of many within the community.[2] Consequently, this strategy participates in the history of biblical

---

An earlier version of this essay can be found under the title "Journey and the Fourth Gospel: A Latino/a Exploration," *Int* 65 (2011): 264–75. That essay builds off a shorter article of mine entitled "The Bible as a Text in Cultures: Latinas/os," in *The Peoples' Bible: New Revised Standard Version with the Apocrypha*, ed. Curtiss Paul DeYoung et al. (Minneapolis: Fortress Press, 2009), 37–43.

1. For an excellent volume that employs this strategy in a critical fashion, see Fleur S. Houston, *You Shall Love the Stranger as Yourself: The Bible, Refugees, and Asylum* (New York: Routledge, 2015).

2. As I will mention below as well, not all Latinos/as see themselves through

interpretation by pointing to the strategy's belongingness, that is, situating it within a broader stream of interpretation,[3] but at the same time the strategy distinguishes itself from other interpretations by offering a particular reading of the plot of the Fourth Gospel.

Introduction

As I have already alluded to, trying to search for one particular hermeneutical strategy that Latinos/as have used or are using to read the Bible is challenging. In fact, it is fruitless because Latinos/as are too diverse even among themselves. Latinos/as come from many corners of Latin America. For instance, their ancestral roots are not all the same, their Spanish and indigenous dialects and foods are not all identical, and even their political worlds or religious worldviews are not all alike. What is more, Latinos/as' histories of colonialization are dissimilar. The colonialization of many countries by the European powers and the United States, not to mention the colonization of Cuba by the former Soviet Union, has left an indelible mark upon the identities and even behaviors, theologies, and religions of Latinos/as in the United States, including the ways that both recent and long-standing Latinos/as' communities read the Bible. As such, the challenge to define or to paint a particular picture of how Latinos/as read or study the Bible would simply be exhausting. The best one can do is to try to cut a large swath in order to get a sense of how Latinos/as read living in a bicultural or multiple worlds (physically and/or metaphorically). This can be done either by examining how they are collectively perceived as Other in society or by trying to draw on a common experience such as the experience of journey or travel.

---

the optic of immigration. Some, particularly Mexican-Americans, have lived in the US Southwest (Arizona, New Mexico, and Texas), California, and other states such as Nevada, Utah, Wyoming, Colorado, and Kansas prior to the territory becoming part of the United States in 1848. See Gonzalez, *Harvest of Empire*, 27–57, 96–107.

3. See my brief ideological-literary reading of John 13:1–11 (foot-washing scene) through the perspective of postcolonial hospitality in "Narrative Identities of the Gospel of John," in *The Oxford Handbook to Biblical Narrative*, ed. Danna Nolan Fewell (Oxford: Oxford University Press, 2015), 341–50.

As such, in this chapter, I aim to focus on the experience of journey or travel or migration (for more recent Latinos/as).[4] In other words, it is the journey that many (not all) Latinos/as take from one country or island to another or the journey that many Latinos/as take traveling to one urban or rural community to another for work within the United States. For instance, many Latinos/as have been displaced or travelled clandestinely due to political laws enacted to return many undocumented Latinos/as to their home countries. Many have travelled to the United States during different periods of history and from a panoply of geographical locations. In fact, many have always lived in the United States, as is the case with generations of Mexican Americans in the Southwest. In this chapter, I wish to explore this experience of journeying as a way to better understand what it means to read the Bible from a bicultural or multicultural perspective. For me, I choose to dwell on this experience of journey because it is still fresh in my memory from witnessing how family members and friends were received, for example, when they arrived from their native homes, but also because the reality still exists today for many Latin Americans and others globally who go through their own respective journeys to the United States and to other countries not their own.[5]

Thus, I aim to bring the experience or reality of journey by many Latin American migrants to the plot of the Fourth Gospel as a sample of how a Latino/a reading might appear for some.[6] The goal here is to correlate the

---

4. The theme of journey and travel is also found in film, such as in the important Latino/a films: Robert M. Young, dir., *Alambrista* (Beverly Hills, CA: Filmhaus, 1979); Gregory Nava, dir., *El Norte* (New York: Public Broadcasting Service, 1984). One can also found find the journey theme in Latino/a literature; see Francisco Jiménez, *The Circuit: Stories from the Life of a Migrant Child* (Albuquerque: University of New Mexico Press, 1997); Julia Ortiz Copher, *The Line of the Sun* (Athens: University of Georgia Press, 1991); Cristina Garcia, *Dreaming in Cuban* (New York: Ballantine, 1993); Julia Álvarez, *How the García Girls Lost Their Accent* (New York: Plume, 1992).

5. For an excellent understanding of the nuances of immigration globally and in relation to its representation in the text, see Houston, *You Shall Love the Stranger*.

6. This hermeneutical move is not without its issues. "Reading for" or "reading with" communities may obfuscate the genuine experiences of the community. In other words, the interpreter's social location is always involved in the process of "reading for" or "reading with" a community.

experience of journey found in the Fourth Gospel with the experience of Latinos/as and to explore the plot in a way that might raise some questions pertaining to the reality of journeying for Latinos/as—not to mention other ethnic/racial communities. This theme of journey is not new to Latino/a hermeneutics. On the contrary, it is quite common. Therefore, before proceeding to the reading of the plot of the Fourth Gospel, I will explore this theme a bit further.

Journeys and Latino/a Hermeneutics

One possible way to begin to explore this reality of journey among Latinos/ as is to examine the various ways Latinos/as have read the Bible through the lens of their journeying experiences and through their cultural experiences as a minoritized community in the United States. I will focus on the experiences of unsettlement, travel/crossing, and resettlement. These experiences are understood broadly. They not only signify an external journey (that is, traveling from home country to host country); they also refer to an internal journey (that is, movement within the host country). Reasons for leaving are many. With regard to external journeys, Latino/a communities leave for a variety of motivations: political reasons (e.g., civil unrest, colonialism), economic reasons (e.g., globalization, scarcity of jobs), cultural reasons (e.g., social migration to reunite with family, religious intolerance), and natural reasons (e.g., earthquakes, hurricanes). Internal journeys are also undertaken for a plethora of reasons: socioeconomic reasons (e.g., searching for jobs), political reasons (anti-immigration laws), cultural reasons (e.g., English-only legislation), and natural reasons (e.g., famines). Journeys have traditionally been viewed in a linear-temporal fashion, assuming that after the experience of resettlement, the travel experience ceases both physically and mentally. Perhaps a more inclusive view would see journey as a circular-temporal event that entails an ongoing experience. In other words, with every new wave of migration from Latin America, the process of journey starts over for that particular travel community and for the Latino/a community overall. In addition, a circular-temporal understanding encompasses the view that journeys occur along the lines of sociopsychology or in the memory of many Latinos/as. This latter occurrence is reflected in the titles of some biblical commentaries and theological books (e.g., *Galilean Journey, Strangers in Our Own Land, A Dream Unfinished*, and *Christians at the Border).*[7] Finally, the construct *journey* is not something fixed and stable but quite fluid and extending beyond the first generations (with lasting effects); even so, it may not be the best reflection of all the experiences of all Latinos/as in the United States.

Unsettlement

In the history of Latinos/as in the United States, many Latin American communities, due to the violent encounter of the Spanish empire in the sixteenth to the eighteenth centuries, as well as the United States' colonial-imperial involvement throughout much of Latin America and the Caribbean from as early as the nineteenth century to the present, experienced the unsettlement and migration of a variety of Latin Americans to and within the United States. In the case of many Latinos/as (Mexicans) in the Southwest of the United States, their political identity changed involuntarily overnight when the United States acquired the Southwest Territory (known by Chicanos/as as *Aztlán*) after the Mexican-US War and the Treaty of Guadalupe Hidalgo in 1848. Similarly, the identity of Puerto Ricans changed to subjects of the United States overnight with the colonization of their island in 1898, resulting in the industrialization of Puerto Rico and the displacement of many rural Puerto Ricans as a result of the US government's economic program called Operation Bootstrap (*Operación Manos a la Obra*) in 1942.[8] This experience of colonialism or neocolonialism led many Latin Americans to unsettle (internally as well as externally) from their homelands to various host countries, including the United States. This experience is characterized as uprootedness, which is reflected in many Latinos/as' reading of the Bible and is part of what is

---

7. See Elizondo, *Galilean Journey*; Hector Avalos, *Strangers in Our Own Land: Religion in U.S. Latina/o Literature* (Nashville: Abingdon Press, 2005); Eleazar S. Fernandez and Fernando F. Segovia, eds., *A Dream Unfinished: Theological Reflections on America from the Margins* (Eugene, OR: Wipf & Stock; 2006); Carroll R., *Christians at the Border.*

8. See Eileen J. Suárez Findlay, *We Are Left without a Father Here: Masculinity, Domesticity, and Migration in Postwar Puerto Rico,* American Encounters/ Global Interactions (Durham, NC: Duke University Press, 2014), who discusses the implications of both the US and Puerto Rican governments' economic policies upon families.

meant by a Latino/a perspective. It is especially visible in the reading strategies, principles, and assumptions of many Latinos/as' biblical readings.

Prior to the 1980s, the traditional academic way to read the Christian Scriptures was to borrow from the long-reigning and heroic model
of historical criticism. Historical criticism, focused primarily on written
and oral sources used by authors and the histories and settings behind
the biblical texts, and the author's special emphases and theologies established a foothold on how to read the Christian Scriptures. It was the way
many Latinos/as, particularly if trained in the United States and Europe
or by institutions in Latin America, informed by historical criticism,
were trained to read the Christian Scriptures. As the US expansionism
increased and spread throughout the nineteenth and twentieth centuries,
so did the approach of historical criticism. However, forces arose that
began to cause unsettlement in the field of biblical studies. Leaving behind
the traditional methods (but not altogether), many Latin Americans (now
Latinos/as) newly arrived in the United States as well as Latinos/as already
in the United States began to depart from the historical critical approach.
It simply was not addressing their questions about the biblical text. Consequently, historical criticism's principles of positivism and universality
began to be challenged, for example, and its notions that meaning is apo-
litical and that the reader is invisible during the reading experience also
began to be abandoned. This departure led many Latinos/as to borrow
from liberation hermeneutics' push to decolonize and contextualize the
experience of the interpreter and reading community.

One of the earliest examples of this is Virgilio Elizondo's *Galilean Journey: A Mexican American Promise*, in which Elizondo, drawing from the
historical, social, and theological experiences of Mexican Americans, reads
the gospels through the experience of *mestizaje*—the cultural and racial
intermixing of the Mexican people due to the cultural (and violent) encounter among the Spanish (Roman Catholic) and the indigenous communities
of the Southwest.[9] Jesus and Mexican Americans, Elizondo argues, are
both *mestizos*. They are both marginalized and outcasts within their societies. Another example is Justo González's strategy of reading "in Spanish"
reflected in his book *Mañana: Christian Theology from a Hispanic Perspec-*

---

9. See Elizondo, *Galilean Journey*. For a more nuanced view of *mestizaje*,
see Néstor Medina, *Mestizaje: (Re)Mapping Race, Culture, and Faith in Latina/o
Catholicism*, Studies in Latino/a Catholicism (Maryknoll, NY: Orbis Books, 2009).

tive, in which González reads the Christian Scriptures from the experience of exile (stranger in a new land) and through the experience of oppression.[10] Both readings are representative of this unsettlement. Latinos/as, dissatisfied with historical criticism's promises of prosperity, stood up and began to travel to a new location. Drawing from this experience of unsettlement, as such, many Latinos/as began to explore where to go next. At the same time, filled with a new consciousness and dissatisfied with where historical critical readings were taking them, they then embarked on retooling and taking the risk of a new journey, back and forth sometimes, to "el norte," across the sea, and crossing the Southwest toward a new terrain in the hope of something new for them and their community.

Travel: Crossing Borders

The experience of crossing borders for Latinos/as is not the same for all. In fact, it is diverse and unique as reflected in the identities of the community. For many it is quite dangerous and for others it is quite safe. Some cross borders because of civil war (e.g., Central Americans, Argentinians), political repression (e.g., Cubans, Dominicans), and economic disparity (Puerto Ricans, Mexicans); some cross borders to rejoin family as many women and children are doing today to join their husbands and fathers who cannot travel back to their home country due to stricter immigration policies. Some Latin Americans even cross because of sexual orientation or transgender identity persecution.[11] Latino/a communities are also further characterized differently by their status. Some are considered migrants (legal or illegal), and others are viewed as political exiles and refugees when crossing borders. Some communities cross the borders of states (e.g., Texas to Oklahoma) as internally displaced migrants, and some cross land, water, and air. Thus, the experience of crossing is distinctive for each of the Latino/a communities in the United States and even diverse within a particular group itself. This experience of journey is characterized by crossing borders (physical and metaphoric), rivers, and waters, and the expereience is reflected in the reading strategies of many Latinos/as of the Bible.

---

10. See Justo L. González, *Mañana: Christian Theology from a Hispanic Perspective* (Nashville: Abingdon, 1990).

11. See Luibhéid and Cantú, *Queer Migrations*; Cantú, *Sexuality of Migration*.

Resettlement

Once in the United States or other receiving country, many Latin Americans (now Latinos/as) must engage the realities of settling into their host state, county, city, and neighborhood. Such resettlement will depend on what stance the host community has adopted toward welcoming newly arrived migrants, as well as how much these migrants wish to assimilate into a community, integrate into a community, or maintain multiple identities in a community.[12] Social factors such as racialization, class, sexual identity, or legal status will influence the attitudes of both the receiving community and the arriving community. For instance, some Latinos/as wish to assimilate into the host community as a way to belong. At the same time, the host community assumes that all who are different ought to assimilate. Such assimilation calls for the migrant, for example, to divest him or herself (themselves) of his or her (their) culture and accept the culture of the host community. Sometimes this is done by assuming Anglicized names (e.g., Roberto to Robert, Margarita to Margaret, or Francisco to Frank), and sometimes this is done by dress or appearance. If they do not assimilate, migrants might not be received well within the host community, and sometimes the host community will indicate their preference through racialized speech or by creating white spatial places where migrants cannot live.[13]

Some Latinos/as wish to integrate into a host community as they resettle. Such integration calls for migrants to maintain their cultural identity and traditions while also conforming to the identity and traditions of their host communities. Such integration also allows the migrant to integrate into the new community politically while the host community aims to extend a space for them to belong within this community. There is less pressure to conform compared to the assimilationist approach, though racialization and other forms of exclusion persist, such as the expectation

---

12. See the excellent volume on international migration by Castles and Miller, *The Age of Migration*, which discusses the community as political body in relationship to citizenship (44–47).

13. For a clear understanding of how white spatial imaginary is created, thus excluding minoritized groups, see George Lipsitz, *How Racism Takes Place* (Philadelphia: Temple University Press, 2011).

that the migrants will relinquish their identity (e.g., citizenship) of the sending country.

Finally, some Latinos/as wish both to maintain their sending country's identity and culture and, at the same time, adapt to their new home community's identity and culture. Such an attitude calls for a bicultural identity in which migrants can belong to both their sending country and their new home country at the same time. Such a position, though, is not often well received by receiving communities, who often call for migrants to learn to speak English only, worship along the lines of Anglo Christianity and in English, and, even cheer only for US international and Olympic teams, as in soccer. The issue of resettlement is one that reflects the lasting effects of journeying from one place to another in the migrant's entire life.

Johannine Travel

Now to correlate this diverse and intricate Latino/a reality of journey (unsettlement, travel/crossing, and resettlement) to the pattern of journey to the Fourth Gospel. The Fourth Gospel commences with a cosmic journey also by way of unsettlement, travel/crossing, and resettlement: unsettlement from above to below (narrative of beginnings, 1:1–18); travel/crossing in four journey cycles from Galilee/Bethany to Jerusalem (narrative of belongingness, 1:19–17:26); and resettlement from below to above with God (narrative of return, 18:1–21:25).[14] The framework for

---

14. This is not the first time that the theme of journey has been explored in the Fourth Gospel. See, for instance, Fernando F. Segovia, "The Journey(s) of the Word of God: A Reading of the Plot of the Fourth Gospel," *Semeia* 53 (1991): 23–54. In this particular reading, I follow the delineation of the narrative structure of the plot of the Fourth Gospel found in Segovia's essay. My narrative reading is also informed by other Johannine studies, such as Leticia A. Guardiola-Sáenz, "Jesus the Borderlander: Hybridity As Survival Strategy and Model for Political Change: A Cultural Representation from the Gospel of John" (PhD diss., Vanderbilt University, 2009); Yak-Hwee Tan, "The Johannine Community: Caught in 'Two Worlds,'" in *New Currents through John: A Global Perspective*, ed. Francisco Lozada Jr. and Tom Thatcher, RBS 54 (Atlanta: Society of Biblical Literature, 2006), 167–79; R. Alan Culpepper, *Anatomy of the Fourth Gospel: A Study of Literary Design* (Philadelphia: Fortress, 1983); Warren Carter, *John and Empire: Initial Explorations* (New York: T&T Clark, 2008); Adele Reinhartz, *Befriending*

this reading of the plot of John emanates from the experience of journey that many Latinos/as (particularly recent groups) have. In addition, the plot is informed by the encounters different characters have centered on the recognition of Jesus's identity as Son of God and the typical identity issues that follow cultural encounters such as belongingness, Otherness, reciprocity of hospitality, and community. The recognition of recent migrant Latinos/as is in a similar (but not identical) way intertwined with others, especially with the host population, through encounters in which they struggle, negotiate, and comply with living in a new community (including ecclesial communities). What follows is a general reading of the plot of the Fourth Gospel, not with the aim of raising intriguing questions about the character of Jesus's journey per se, but rather with the aim of raising thought-provoking questions about the reality of journey for many Latinos/as today as well as others.[15]

Narrative of Beginnings (1:1-18)

The start of the journey for the character of Jesus begins in the Prologue (1:1-18). As is well attested, the Prologue is a prolepsis of the journey(s) Jesus takes throughout the plot of the Fourth Gospel. The Prologue, as such, provides glimpses of the various encounters Jesus experiences in the plot of the Fourth Gospel. In some encounters, Jesus is received well by strangers and friends, but in others he is rejected by others and his very own community. At the end he returns home to be with his cosmic family, leaving his identity through the Spirit with his family below.

The Prologue can be divided into three sections: the beginning of the journey from above (1:1-13), the journey to the world below (1:14-17),

---

the Beloved Disciple: A Jewish Reading of the Gospel of John (New York: Continuum, 2001); Jeffrey L. Staley and Musa W. Dube, eds., John and Postcolonialism: Travel, Space and Power, Bible and Postcolonialism 7 (Sheffield: Sheffield Academic, 2002).

15. The former aim to examine the journey of Jesus in the Fourth Gospel from a literary point of view is quite important and a task I leave for another time. Some earlier thoughts on the plot, which I still rely on, can be found in Francisco Lozada Jr., A Literary Reading of John 5: Text as Construction (New York: Lang, 2000), 50-57.

and the return journey to home above (1:18).[16] As such, Jesus, one could argue, is on a journey narrated in the Prologue and throughout the Fourth Gospel. The first part of the journey focuses on the Word's beginnings, with information regarding the Word's context. The Word existed in the beginning, the Word is with God, and the Word is God (1:1–2). Thus, the Prologue commences with temporal, spatial, and relational information about the identity of Jesus. The Prologue continues the Word's journey, but this journey moves away from the Word's relationship with God toward one between the Word and the world below. Consequently, the journey begins with the Word's relationship to creation (1:3) and the Word's relationship to humanity (1:4–13). In this relationship, the journey discloses that the Word is the source of life and light and not darkness (1:4), that the Word is confirmed, by John the Baptist, as the one sent from God (1:5–9) and not by humans, and that the Word will be received by some and rejected by others (1:10–13). The journey is thus one where the identity of the Word is introduced as one who lives on the "frontier" between two distinct and opposed communities: a community that recognizes and believes in the identity of the Word as God and a community that does not recognize and believe (1:1).

In the second section of the Prologue, the Word journeys to the world below (1:14–17). The Word becomes flesh (human) and lives among those in the world below. Unlike those who did not receive Jesus as the Word, those who did receive the Word experienced or found grace and truth in the Word (1:14b). They also found glory in the Word (1:14c). Just because the Word became flesh (human), the Word did not cease to be divine (glory), since this notion of glory comes from God (1:14d). Adding support to this claim, the journey introduces John the Baptist once more and draws upon the Jewish tradition of Moses as a witness to the identity of Jesus as the Word (1:15–17). The journey to the world below thus confirms Jesus's identity as one who travels or one who journeys to a new world. Yet, unlike a recently arrived migrant from Latin America who has entered the United States, Jesus's experience bears little resemblance to the reality a migrant might experience in his or her new world. Jesus knows the language and cultural codes and how to navigate through the political and

---

16. See Fernando F. Segovia, "John 1:1–18 as Entrée into Johannine Reality," in *Word, Theology, and Community in John*, ed. John Painter, R. Alan Culpepper, and Fernando F. Segovia (St. Louis: Chalice, 2002), 33–64.

religious institutions of the world he crosses over into. For many Latino/a migrants or Latinos/as in general in the United States, learning how to negotiate between two worlds, the world they are familiar with and the world they are not, is a constant challenge.

The journey ceases in the Prologue with Jesus as the Word returning to the world above with God (1:18). Jesus returns and makes his mission known to the world below, but he also reduces his identity in the narrowest way by calling for the reader (or hearer) to make a choice to receive Jesus as the Word and the Son of God or not. Such either/or choices can be challenging to Latinos/as who are called often to make a choice of allegiance between home or host country—a choice that can lead to lasting fear or bitterness toward one's host country or a choice that can lead to vitriolic laws imposed upon the Latino/a community.[17]

Narrative of Belongingness (1:19–17:26)

In the next division (1:19–17:26), Jesus's journey can be delineated into a fourfold Galilee/Jerusalem cycle: first journey (1:19–3:36), second journey (4:1–5:47), third journey (6:1–10:42), and final journey (11:1–17:26).[18] All four journeys involve travel between Galilee and Jerusalem, with transitional sections set in locations between the two main locations, such as Judea and Bethany. All of the journeys entail two major communities: one community that shows a need to belong to the world above (believers) and another that shows its need to belong to the world below (unbelievers) as set forth in the plot of the Fourth Gospel. It is a plot that reflects a similar reality among Latinos/as and recent migrants today who struggle with the

---

17. An example is the 2010 anti-immigration bill from Arizona entitled Arizona Senate Bill 1070, which considers it a crime (misdemeanor) for an undocumented person to live in Arizona without the required documents in possession. In Texas (i.e., the suburb of Farmers Branch) and throughout the country (e.g., Hazelton, Pennsylvania; Escondido, California), local governments have attempted to pass housing laws such as one requiring proof of citizenship to rent or own a home. See Caroline B. Brettell and Faith G. Nibbs, "Immigrant Suburban Settlement and the 'Threat' to Middle Class Status and Identity: The Case of Farmers Branch, Texas," International Migration 49 (2011): 1–30.

18. See Segovia, "Journey(s) of the Word."

notion of belongingness—a plot that is also visible among many groups in the history of immigration to the United States.[19]

First Journey (1:19–3:36)

The first journey (1:19–3:36) begins with John the Baptist testifying to the identity of Jesus as the Lamb of God (1:19–34), followed by Jesus calling upon disciples to follow him during his journey to Cana in Galilee. It is here in Cana that Jesus's own allegiances are challenged (2:1–12). Jesus must decide whether to honor his mother's request to perform a miracle (changing water into wine) (2:3c) or to honor God's request: "My hour has not yet come" (2:4c NRSV). It is a struggle between the world below (the need to maintain his mother's honor at the wedding) and the world above (the need to obey God's plan). Jesus fulfills both needs by honoring his mother and God. His fulfillment raises questions about reciprocity of hospitality toward the stranger, which perhaps is a direction that needs further exploration even if the exploration leads to an unsatisfactory end.

The first journey continues with Jesus heading to Jerusalem (2:13–3:36). On this journey, Jesus threatens to destroy the temple and supersede it (2:13–25), and he encounters Nicodemus the Pharisee contending that one must be born again or anew (world above) to receive salvation (3:16). The journey transitions into the countryside of Judea where Jesus and John once more confirm Jesus's identity as the Son of God/Christ (3:22–30): "You yourselves are my witnesses that I said, 'I am not the Messiah, but I have been sent ahead of him'" (3:28 NRSV). During Jesus's journey to Jerusalem, Jesus's allegiance to the world above is clear, despite differences that exist in the world below. Ironically, when Jesus's allegiance to the world above is challenged or contested, as occurred during his journey to Jerusalem, he finds it necessary to defend it. Such a hostile reaction toward Jesus underscores the challenges Latinos/as endure when their sense of belonging in the United States is also challenged and attacked.

---

19. To understand how the issue of belongingness has been at the forefront of many migrant groups' relationships with many Anglo-American-controlled institutions, see Natalia Molina, *How Race Is Made in America: Immigration, Citizenship, and the Historical Power of Racial Scripts*, American Crossroads 38 (Berkeley: University of California Press, 2014). Molina focuses on the period 1924–1965.

This defensive reaction is one that needs further understanding rather than immediate dismissal.

Second Journey (4:1–5:47)

The second journey begins in Judea and has Galilee as its immediate goal, a journey that requires Jesus to pass through the region of Samaria. Here Jesus enters into an unfamiliar region, tired, according to the plot, and encounters a Samaritan woman at a well (4:1–6). The woman is drawing water, and Jesus then engages her by asking her for a drink of water. This request for water will lead to several discourses between the woman and Jesus. First, the plot points out the difference between Jesus and the Samaritan on several fronts. The Samaritan woman questions how Jesus, a Jew, could ask her for a drink, thus pointing out the ethnic/racial Otherness of both. The Samaritan woman also points out a gender Otherness; namely, she is a woman alone with a man, Jesus, at the well—a cultural taboo. She points out that Jews had no dealings with Samaritans, so the encounter is distinct on many levels. The dialogue continues and centers on the identity of Jesus as the living water (4:7–15). The Samaritan woman, although not believing at first, ultimately believes in Jesus as the source of eternal life and goes off to share her new knowledge with her community (4:16–26). The journey is thus one where cultural and gender encounters between the Samaritan woman and Jesus reveal vast differences between two characters, but it is also one where the encounter will lead to a different level of relationship. Whereas both were quite foreign to one another on several levels, it is the Samaritan woman who makes an interesting move toward understanding who Jesus is. Jesus always remains the same (static) in the plot of the Fourth Gospel.[20] The characters Jesus engages with are the ones who make changes. The interesting move is that the Samaritan woman aims to understand Jesus by moving closer to his culture (belief), but one wonders whether Jesus, in the plot, moves closer to her culture. Jesus's allegiance is to God, to the world above, and God appears to have a plan for him (2:4; 7:30; 8:20). On a cultural level, the Samaritan woman shows or hints that by moving away from her culture and beliefs toward belief in Jesus, she has taken a step

---

20. See Culpepper, *Anatomy of the Fourth Gospel*, 106–12.

toward understanding the Other (Jesus). On the other hand, the question is whether Jesus the character is willing to move away from his culture and beliefs and thus willing to understand her culture without her giving up any of her beliefs. The story of the Samaritan woman and Jesus thus brings to the forefront the question of respect and reciprocity, which is found in many of the journeys of migrants who face tensions of belongingness in the host country. How much of one's culture must be respected for the migrant to reciprocate such respect? More specifically, how much of their culture must a Latino/a give up to retain a sense of belongingness in the United States, even after having been residents of the United States for many years?

The second journey in the Fourth Gospel continues with Jesus performing another miracle in Cana, but this time the miracle is done from a distance (4:46–54). The miracle involves a Roman official in Judea, according to the plot, whose son is ill in Capernaum. The official goes to Cana to ask Jesus for a miracle, and because of the official's strong faith in Jesus, the son is healed. On his way to Jerusalem, Jesus performs another miracle, healing a lame man at a pool in Jerusalem (5:1–9a). The healing takes place on the Sabbath, which leads to a dialogue between Jesus and the Jews. The end result is a threat on Jesus's life and Jesus calling God his Father (5:16–18). The chapter concludes with a long discourse or monologue centered on Jesus's identity as the Son of God, thus confirming his authority and power to heal (5:19–47).

The plot during this second journey cycle surely casts Jesus as one who engages various characters: the Samaritan woman, the Roman official, the lame man, and even the Jews. In all such engagements, the characters have either to come to believe in Jesus or are cast as unbelievers. If Jesus is the center of the cosmos, it is the responsibility of the characters to come to the center to receive the rewards for such belief. The point here is that the plot of the Fourth Gospel raises important questions for Latinos/as about the dynamics and ramifications of coming to the center when the perceived center is not always welcoming or hospitable.

Third Journey (6:1–10:42)

The third journey takes up more of the plot of the Fourth Gospel. Beginning in Galilee, Jesus performs another miracle of feeding five thousand (6:1–15), a theophany by way of walking on water (6:16–21), and a long

discourse leading to calling himself the Bread of Life (6:22–71). The journey culminates in Galilee with some of Jesus's close friends not believing
in him as the Bread of Life (7:1–9). Similar to John 2:1–12, Jesus is not
ready, particularly during the Feast of Tabernacles, to show himself openly
to the world, for his hour has not yet come (7:6). The plot plays with the
theme of secrecy here, as it did earlier in the plot with Nicodemus, thus
raising questions about the secrecy of identity during journeys; similarly,
many newly arrived Latinos/as live in secrecy today as a result of their
undocumented status in the United States.

Once in Jerusalem for a third time, a series of events unfolds
(7:10–10:39). First, Jesus appears in the temple teaching and providing
a "counterreading" of the Torah during the Feast of Tabernacles, which
leads to threats of arrest as well as threats on his life; he then concludes
with another reading of the Scriptures on the last day of the festival, with
some believing in him and others remaining in unbelief (7:10–44). Other
important events occur on this journey, though most fail to believe, with
the exception of the blind man (9:1–41). While still in Jerusalem, Jesus
heals a blind man, who gradually comes to believe in (see) Jesus as the
Son of God. However, his parents, the crowd, and the Jews all fail to be
convinced that Jesus brought sight to the once blind man. The irony here,
as is well attested, is that the man born blind comes to see, whereas those
who can see are willfully blind to Jesus's true identity. The story surely calls
into question nativist discourses used today in the United States by people
who are "blind" to their own respective migrant origins.

Jesus reaffirms his identity through a figurative discourse of the shepherd and the sheep (10:1–42). Jesus is cast as the shepherd who calls his
sheep by name (10:3). Those who believe in Jesus recognize his voice and
follow him, whereas those who fail to believe follow the paths of others,
such as the thief, bandit, hirelings, and wolves. The Jews, also failing to
believe (according to the story), make another attempt to arrest Jesus. This
third journey cycle ends with Jesus retreating across the Jordan to avoid
arrest. During his sojourn there, many come to believe in him.

The plot of the third journey includes many events. One element that
stands out in the context and experience of journey is the attempt to
mark some differences between the believers and the unbelievers and to
establish some borders between them. Journeys can do this, but they can
also challenge these borders between communities by aiming to reduce
differences and abolish those frontiers, but only when there is respect for

one another. The plot of the third journey raises this question once again of reciprocity. Does Jesus as character aim to understand others' points of view, and do the others aim to understand Jesus's point of view? The plot does not help when it calls on characters to believe or not believe in Jesus. It places the characters in a box with no room to maneuver. Such a binary choice is one that many migrants (and Latinos/as) face during their own journey as members of a community. The ideology of binary constructs forces migrants to see community as a matter of belonging or not, of being seen as human or not, rather than seeing community as bifurcated and seeing the possibility of moving in and out of one community.

Fourth Journey (11:1–17:26)

The fourth journey begins in the region of Judea and the village of Bethany and ends in Jerusalem (11:1–17:26). While in Bethany, Jesus heals Lazarus at the request of both Martha and Mary (11:1–44). Although the healing of Lazarus from death to life is successful, the rest of the scene is marked by the continual division among the Jews over the identity of Jesus (11:45–46). The end result is pivotal, in that the chief priests and the Pharisees finally decide to put Jesus to death because of the healing of Lazarus (11:46–12:11). When Jesus enters Jerusalem for the last time, the authorities are still apparently divided in their belief regarding Jesus's true identity (12:12–50). While having a final farewell dinner with his disciples, Jesus exposes and expels his betrayer (13:26–27), who has given Jesus up to the authorities for death. Jesus concludes the journey with a farewell prayer to God, calling for the unity of all.

In this farewell prayer (17:1–26), Jesus turns away from speaking to the disciples to speak to God, the heavenly Father, in the world above. The prayer begins with Jesus offering himself as a sacrifice to the Father (17:1–5), followed by a request or plea to the Father for the protection of his disciples (17:6–19), and concludes with Jesus asking for the unity of the universal community for those who believe even beyond the present age (17:20–26). In other words, it is a prayer of salvation for the present and future community of believers. However, this unity comes with certain ramifications. These are ramifications that call for a faith that transcends regional and social commitments as a way of belonging to the world above—one must be born anew. Is this what the plot of the Fourth Gospel is calling for? The plot, therefore, questions once again what is at stake when one assimilates into a host community. Is it necessary to give up distinctive linguistic, cultural, and social factors to become like the central group (believers) of the plot? Similarly, this is a very real question facing many Latinos/as today in the United States. How much of my identity do I have to give up in order to belong in the United States?

Narrative of Return (18:1–21:25)

The Fourth Gospel concludes with Jesus's journey in Jerusalem and beyond (18:1–21:25). Jesus is arrested, appears before the Jewish and gentile authorities, and then dies on the cross and appears to his disciples by the Sea of Tiberias. At the end, Jesus, the Word, returns to the world above to be with God, returning unchanged, though leaving his Spirit/influence behind. Jesus the character returns home unchanged, unlike many Latinos/as, particularly migrant Latinos/as, who return to their home country very much changed and often not for the better.

Conclusion

The plot, overall, raises questions or glimpses into important questions about the experience and reality of journey. In other words, the reality that many migrants endure during their journey is not only a physical one that often endangers their safety but also a sociopsychological one, in that migrant journeys also take place in the memories of many Latinos/as—as with many groups journeying from one place to another—and continue to play in the interactions between the Latino/a community overall and the dominant Anglo community in the United States. This is a reality that I suspect also takes place in religious communities. To understand the reality that the plot reveals, at least for me, is to unravel those dichotomous constructs that pit groups against one another. Reciprocal hospitality is perhaps something to explore further, since the plot of the Fourth Gospel touches on it throughout.[21] The host community must respect the culture of the Other; likewise, the Other must respect the culture of the host community. The plot of the Fourth Gospel leaves no doubt that this task is not

---

21. See n. 3.

an easy one, for even the character of Jesus constantly has to negotiate living in the world during his own particular journey; yet unlike Latinos/as, the Johannine Jesus is in a position of privilege in those negotiations, whereas many migrants (especially the poor) are not.

The strategy of correlation functions here to highlight the intentions of the plot of the Fourth Gospel, but it does so in a way that might relate it to the experience of migrants. In other words, the strategy allows for the experience of Latino/a migrants to emerge in a way that brings out aspects of the plot that have not been seen by others and facets of the Latino/a migrant experience that are not understood or known. This approach is not without its limitations,[22] as all approaches are, but this one aims to maintain continuity between the text and the lives of its readers, with the goal of providing a new vision of hope for its readers and, consciously or unconsciously, providing a different reading of the Fourth Gospel. The more readings we have that challenge binary plots such as the one reflected in the Fourth Gospel, the less likely that the binary plot can close the text and establish finite readings.[23] This latter assertion on my part extends to migrants in the United States as well, who often find themselves trapped in a stark binary world of legal/illegal. The more readings of their stories and experiences of journeying there are, the greater the disruption of any dichotomous rendering of who they are, thus keeping their identities in flux while seeking belongingness.

---

22. For an excellent review of the hermeneutical issues related to contextual approaches, see Fernando F. Segovia, "Reading Across: Intercultural Criticism and Textual Posture," in *Interpreting beyond Borders*, ed. Fernando F. Segovia, Bible and Postcolonialism 3 (Sheffield Academic, 2000), 59–83.

23. Houston, *You Shall Love the Stranger*, 3.

4

Matthew 6:9b-13 (The Lord's Prayer): A Dialogical Strategy

In the previous chapter I aimed to demonstrate how a correlation strategy might function when applied to a text. This approach related the issues of the interpreter or community (e.g., journeys by migrants) to the issues of the text by foregrounding the thematic element of journey reflected in the story and structure of the Fourth Gospel. Taking a slightly different turn, this chapter will apply a dialogical strategy to a text, the Lord's Prayer (Matt 6:9b-13).[1] The dialogical strategy presumes (similar to the correlation strategy) that the text can instigate a discussion of a particular issue

---

An earlier version of most of the material contained in this revised and updated interpretative chapter is published under the title "Matthew 6:9b-13 (The Lord's Prayer): Explorations into a Latino/a Optic on Language and Translation," in *Matthew*, ed. Nicole Wilkinson Duran and James Grimshaw, Texts @ Contexts (Minneapolis: Fortress, 2013), 271-85.

1. The Gospel of Luke (11:2-4) and the Didache (8.2) also contain the Lord's Prayer. The latter version includes a doxology. Both versions are dated between the late first century and the early second century. Attention to redaction history or sources (Jewish) of this prayer, which are important to understanding all of the variations of the historical identity of the Lord's Prayer, is not the focus of this chapter. Also, the title "Lord's Prayer" is employed throughout the chapter. This designation emanates from the early church leader Cyprian, who used the Latin title *Oratio dominica*. Another designation, one that I am more familiar with, is *Pater noster* or "Our Father." See Jeffrey B. Gibson, *The Disciples' Prayer: The Prayer Jesus Taught in Its Historical Setting* (Minneapolis: Fortress, 2015), 2 n. 2. Gibson actually refers to the "Lord's Prayer" or the "Our Father" as the "Disciple's Prayer," pointing less to the narrative speaker and more to the tradition from which the prayer emerges, namely, the Matthean church (*Disciples' Prayer*, 8).

that pertains to the social location of the interpreter or community. Where a dialogical strategy differs from a strategy of correlation is that, as I see it, a dialogical strategy approaches the text without the assumption that it can directly equate the reader's situation with the situation of the text—or the situation of the Matthean Jesus in this chapter's case—as in the strategy of correlation. Rather, the text functions more like a dialogue partner who engages the reader in conversation, with one or the other partner evoking a topic or theme as a mode of entry for a conversation. However, all of this is to say that, just because a text does not speak directly to contemporary issues, that does not mean that a text cannot be employed to start a conversation that might lead to the speakers understanding themselves and their situation a bit clearer. In what follows, I draw on Matt 6:9b–13 (the Lord's Prayer) and the topic of language, translation, and interpretation, which helps me (and hopefully others) to understand a bit of the text's Otherness, but likely says more about the translator himself and his community. Such an aim does not "distort" the interpretation; rather, I see Latino/a hermeneutics (like all hermeneutical approaches) strongly influencing how societies see Latino/a communities and how societies interact with or treat them. In this way, the following Latino/a reading of Matthew's Lord's Prayer is in keeping with the history of biblical interpretation's practice of seeing text as a conversation; it belongs, but it also sets itself apart with its particular attention to language, translation, and interpretation.

Introduction

The call to speak only one language, that is, English, in the United States is a call to solve the so-called problem of foreignness or multiple languages in the country. It is a call to conform to the dominant way of life. For many US citizens, one language unites the multiplicity of ethnic/racial groups across the country into one nation mirroring the dominant, Anglo-speaking community. Such a call for assimilation is typically targeted toward Latinos/as who comprise the largest non-English linguistic group in the United States.[2] This push for a monolingual nation influenced some to push for an

---

2. See chapter 12, "Speak Spanish, You're in America! *El Huracán* over Language and Culture," in Gonzalez, *Harvest of Empire*, 225–48.

English-only constitutional amendment and policies. The objective of this push for a monolingual nation is to compel, consciously or unconsciously, all ethnic/racial groups to melt into the "mainstream" of society faster, learn one narrative of US history, and preserve the dominant culture's way of life. What is significant for this chapter's purposes is that advocates for a monolingual nation work with a model of communication that does not allow the Other (e.g., Latinos/as) to speak or exist. It is a model of communication that is unidirectional (conform to me and my way of reading the event) and is driven by strong Enlightenment principles, such as positivism, objectivity, and universalism. The model is more like a monologue than a dialogue between two conversational partners. What I propose is a model of communication that is multidirectional, allowing both partners to learn from one another, not with the intent to conform to one another's perspectives, but with the objective of understanding one another and with the hope that a community allows for differentiated forms of belonging and speaking the language of their choice. By extension, how one communicates in the real world is often "translated" or influences the way one reads texts.[3] Thus, it is this latter communication model (i.e., multidirectional), which aims to take seriously both dialogue partners (e.g., the reader and text in this case), that undergirds my discussion with Matt 6:9b-13, via the optic of language, translation, and interpretation. In other words, this chapter explores the interaction of the role of the reader and text (Matt 6:9b-13) with an eye toward looking at these communication components in constructing meaning.

Why the Lord's Prayer in Matthew? The Lord's Prayer is a text I use at times in a pedagogical context to discuss the development of New Testament methods.[4] It is often studied as having a *problem*; namely, the problem is that it is an ancient foreign-language text that needs to be trans-

---

3. See the chapter "Reading the Bible in Spanish," in González, *Mañana*, 75–87.

4. I have always found the discussion of methods, using the Lord's Prayer as the sample text, in Dennis C. Duling and Norman Perrin, *The New Testament: Proclamation and Parenesis, Myth and History*, 3rd ed. (New York: Harcourt, Brace, 1994), very helpful for teaching the history of approaches to introductory New Testament students. Much of my analysis of the Lord's Prayer is dependent upon this introductory text. For an excellent volume on the history of the Lord's Prayer, see also Gibson, *Disciples' Prayer*.

lated into the vernacular to be understood. In other words, what do the words really mean? Translation is a task that aims to make the strange familiar. However, rather than seeing the text as a problem, approaching the text as a cultural Other with something to contribute is an alternative option that perhaps might render a more faithful translation. Such an alternative objective can be achieved many ways, but I will aim to do so with a close reading of the Lord's Prayer, with attention to its design, individual words, and syntax, and I defer[5] discussion about its composition history, sources, redaction, or other historical or literary readings of it (knowing full well that such reading, again, might say less about the text than about the interpreter).

This reading of Matthew's Lord's Prayer is divided into two major parts. The first part focuses on the context of the reader from the perspective of language, translation, and interpretation. A key factor associated with translation is the element of language and interpretation. As the maxim goes, translating language (and culture) is interpretation. Likewise, translating this reader is an interpretation. The second part examines the design, vocabulary, and syntax of the text. With both components (reader and text), such exploration is partial, a glimpse into both components' identities. My fundamental concern here is to explore the intersection between an aspect of the reader's identity—language, translation, and interpretation—and the same aspect of the text's identity. This reading of the Lord's Prayer is experimental in nature, in that it represents an initial examination of the dialogical approach with a focus on the reader and the text in the reading process. At the same time, the prayer captures well a strategy, for Latinos/as and others, for how to live in a world where dualities aim to conform Latinos/as to speak, translate, and interpret in accord with the dominant culture.

Context of the Reader

As someone who was born in the United States and whose parents migrated to the United States from Puerto Rico (a colonized nation of the United States where Spanish is dominant), I know that language, transla-

---

5. Such deferment, I am fully aware, does not allow the text to speak completely.

tion, and interpretation remain issues of identification for me as well as for others. I and other Latinos/as are not alone on this issue. Many other cultural communities, past and future, whose first language is not English—now the lingua franca of the globalized world—may also resonate with language, translation, and interpretation issues. In my particular case, my first language is now English, yet my subconscious is still colored by Spanish (e.g., I occasionally dream, sing, speak, and write in Spanish). Even so, a mispronunciation of either English or Spanish words points away from the notion of originality or "native" speech or language. Among native English speakers, my various mispronunciations of English words throughout my life have pointed to my Latino identity as not belonging in the United States. Similarly, among native Spanish speakers, my pronunciation and dialect of Spanish point to my being other than a "native" of Latin America. This is not unique to my situation, since language and speech (accents) that are not considered "standard" in many societies across the globe serve as a foundation to locate and identify individuals. In this light, the considerations and meanings associated with language and translation can be quite complex and are often intertwined with identity and how identity is interpreted.

From Subject to Object: Language and Translation

As one who learned and spoke Spanish from a very early age but who, through extreme assimilation, lost much of that language skill, the intersection of language and translation has always been a vital factor of my identity.[6] Specifically, as my communities (i.e., the United States and Latin America) often use language as a placeholder or identifier of cultural or ethnic membership, I am often perceived as an Other. Again, this is true for many peoples who live in more than one cultural, ethnic, national, or even racial milieu due to voluntary or forced migrations. Indeed, choosing which language one speaks at home—whether it is the language of

---

6. In my particular case, both paternal and maternal grandparents arrived in the United States from Puerto Rico with all siblings in the 1950s, with one set of grandparents returning and another remaining. This experience is not unique. It is reflected among many US Puerto Rican families. Language and translation surely played a role in the crossing of cultural, economic, and political boundaries on a daily basis.

one's parents or the language of the larger society—is part of the process of translating and interpreting the identity of the speaker as insider, outsider, or both.

Similarly, when I am in various Latino/a or Latin American communities, whether I choose to speak Spanish or not has outcomes for the perception of my identity. In other words, as a result of my choice of language, someone is translating and interpreting something about me. I have noted that this is also true if I do not speak Spanish in the "right" way. I recognize this reality when someone of Latin American descent tells me that I speak like a "gringo," indicating that I am different from them and from other native speakers.[7] Likewise, some of my family in Puerto Rico have cast me, at one time, as one who does not care about the language and now identifies me as an "Americano" (US American).[8] In the past, I translated and interpreted such comments by others as negative statements and indicators of one or more of my identities. For instance, I felt that they identified me as one who was too lazy to learn my parents' language (or who had parents who were too lazy to teach me). Thus, both groups (native English speakers and native Spanish speakers) worked with a dualistic worldview that required one to conform to speaking only one language. In my case, I chose English with the aim to reach a middle-class identity by way of full assimilation.[9]

This is no longer the case, since I have "detranslated" such comments; that is, I have refused this particular interpretation of my identity. Even so, I know that I am constantly and consistently transformed from a subject to an object. The transformation from subject to object may also be experienced by a non-Spanish-speaking US Latino/a who goes to Latin America and finds himself or herself (themselves) translated from a US Latino/a to an Anglo, or even by a US Latino/a with little command of Spanish who finds oneself identified by others in the community as not "really" a Latino/a. These are the realities of migration, globalization, and

---

7. The term *gringo* refers to Anglo Americans. See Ilan Stavans, *Spanglish: The Making of a New American Language* (New York: HarperCollins, 2003), 136.

8. Depending on the context, the term *Americano/a* in my household referred either to Anglo Americans in general or to those Anglo Americans living the "American Dream" of cultural, economic, and political power.

9. A similar narrative is reflected in Richard Rodriguez, *Hunger of Memory: The Education of Richard Rodriguez; An Autobiography* (New York: Bantam, 1982).

imperialism and the resultant negative impacts these factors have on community members' identities. In turn, these negative impacts leave many
communities, from Argentina to Mexico, lost in translation. The reality
is that we are always translating something or someone from subject to
object—as I myself do when I translate others and when I translate biblical texts like the Lord's Prayer.

Hierarchy of Language

The process of translation is associated with language, which typically has
a hierarchical structure. In other words, similar to class, ethnicity/race,
and nationality, language exists in a perceived hierarchy. This is evidenced
within the English language. For example, those who speak closer to the
"proper" English of England are considered closer to the original language
and people. Also, proper English is associated with the Ivy League New
England dialect, which itself implies a host of social locations, including being more cultured, having higher levels of education, and being
connected to the "established" northeastern families that can trace their
lineage back to the colonial period. Conversely, those who speak what is
considered nonstandard US English are likely to be associated with lower
levels of education, urban and rural communities, the regionalism of the
South, recent migrants, and less established or less notable families. Likewise, in Spanish, those who speak the "authentic" Spanish (Castilian) of
Spain are closer to the top of the hierarchy of language. I suspect this is
illustrative of other languages as well in Great Britain, South Africa, and
the Philippines, to name a few.

   Among US Latinos/as, whose immediate roots are primarily from
Latin America, those who speak closer to the "proper" Spanish language
of Latin America's primary colonizer, Spain, are perceived as closer to
Spain than to their Latin American identity—even though those dialects
of Spanish in Latin America are products of the historical colonization of
the territory and its indigenous and African populations.[10] In this way,
the meanings of language, or the ways in which the uses of language are

---

10. See Giorgio Perissinotto, "Linguistic Constraints, Programmatic Fit, and
Political Correctness: The Case of Spanish in the United States" in *Critical Latin
American and Latino Studies*, ed. Juan Poblete, Cultural Studies of the Americas
12 (Minneapolis: University of Minnesota Press, 2003), 171–87.

socially translated, become part of the domination of a subject—in turn dictating its transformation into an object. In essence, this is a method of achieving control of populations via the process of translating the language, culture, and texts of a given people and then assigning these factors to a very low status level in the social hierarchy. The act of translation and interpretation, then, as with the case of geographical landscape and texts, "is an act of desacralizing"—an act akin to those found in the colonial histories of Australia, Ireland, New Zealand, Nigeria, and even the United States, where mapping became the necessary adjunct of English, French, and Spanish imperialism over the indigenous and other colonized people.[11] Similarly, language and translation in New Testament studies also exists in a perceived hierarchy, with classical or Attic Greek perceived as closer to the ancient Greek culture when compared to the Hellenistic or Koine Greek. Even in the field of biblical studies, the formal correspondence approach, which aims to capture in the translation process the one-to-one correspondence of words from the ancient language to the vernacular, is perceived as closer to the original text's meaning compared to the dynamic approach, which aims to capture the idea behind a word.[12] So even the way in which the text is translated is based on a hierarchical system that has implications regarding the merit and quality of the translation.

Translator

The act of translating a language always involves a translator. The translator is always involved—consciously or unconsciously—in "false" (as some would say) or alternative translations. For instance, the most famous translator in Latin American history was La Malinche (also known as Malintzin, Malinalli, or Doña Marina), who served as a Nahua translator for Hernán Cortéz and the Spanish conquistadores. Cortez relied on her for understanding almost everything about the native Costal Gulf peoples of Mexico that he encountered.[13] Unfortunately, at times, she has

11. See Robert J. C. Young, *Postcolonialism: A Very Short Introduction* (Oxford: Oxford University Press, 2003), 141; Stavans, *Spanglish*, 35.

12. See Peter Kevern, "Translation Theory," in *Searching for Meaning: An Introduction to Interpreting the New Testament*, ed. Paula Gooder (Louisville: Westminster John Knox, 2009), 56–62.

13. See Stavans, *Spanglish*, 25.

been portrayed as a traitor, hence her name La Malinche ("unpatriotic Mexican").[14] Indeed, the act of translation is an act of treachery, as the Italian phrase *traduttore traditore* ("the translator is a traitor") suggests. However, La Malinche performed her translations by representing her own culture that was once removed by language from the indigenous culture; nonetheless hers was a translation and interpretation of the Spanish she heard. Her role is similar to the role of Sacagawea, who served as translator for Lewis and Clark in the eighteenth century. One can find many similar reports of translators and translations with only a cursory examination of the history of the French and the Spaniards in North America. Whether it is an act of diplomacy, treachery, or resistance, translations open up space for the appropriation of a conquering culture; at the same time, translations are dialogues—bringing two cultures together.[15]

Both of the previously mentioned women are no different from any of us who play the role of translator, whether translating the spoken word or written text. We are once or twice removed from the original but nonetheless provide translations and interpretations—albeit ones that are filtered through the particular lenses of our own historical periods and cultural contexts. In the specific case of the Latino/a experience, translations and interpretations can vary depending upon factors such as generation, ethnic background, and geographical location in the United States, to name a few. Also, as mentioned earlier, Latinos/as may speak a Spanish dialect considered by the "old guard" of the language to be nonstandard—one that reflects their regional home country rather than Latin America or Spain more broadly.[16] For better or worse, the Spanish dialect in all its formations exists in a perceived hierarchy, just as Latinos/

---

14. Ibid., 168.

15. See R. S. Sugirtharajah, "Blotting the Master's Copy: Locating Bible Translations," in *Postcolonial Criticism and Biblical Interpretation* (Oxford: Oxford University Press, 2002), 155–78. See also Sugirtharajah, "Textual Cleansings: A Move from the Colonial to the Postcolonial Version," *Semeia* 76 (1996): 7–19. See also, Virginia Burrus, "Augustine's Bible," in *Ideology, Culture, and Translation*, ed. Scott S. Elliott and Roland Boer, SemeiaSt 69 (Atlanta: Society of Biblical Literature, 2012), 69–82.

16. The guard I am referring to is the Real Academia Española de la Lengua Castellana founded in 1713. See Stavans, *Spanglish*, 28–35.

as themselves are categorized within a perceived hierarchy within and outside their own communities.

Thus, all Spanish-speaking people in the United States are engaged in several concurrent acts of translation. Each individual translates and interprets the world, while they are simultaneously being translated by their pan-Latino/a constituencies and by the dominant English-speaking constituencies. For instance, the dialects of recent migrants from less-developed countries in Latin America are typically perceived by many (not all) Spanish teachers in the classroom to be informal or incorrect Spanish (read: not the Spanish spoken in Spain). These teachers then mistakenly attempt to teach the migrant group members as if they were Anglo speakers and not heritage speakers. Heritage speakers are Latinos/as whose ancestors spoke Spanish at one time or whose aural skills are stronger than their oral skills. They may leave certain letters out of their pronunciations (e.g., *eta* for *esta*, which is very typical of my mother's Spanish dialect)[17] and misspell words (e.g., *poyo* for *pollo*) or use words in what is sometimes called Spanglish—the mixing of Spanish and English words in conversation in the United States (e.g., *washeteria, parquear, rentar*). These individuals are frequently judged by their pronunciations and writing skills rather than their intellect, so they are often perceived as "weak" speakers. In other words, heritage speakers are perceived as having a lack of literacy and thus are constantly corrected for their use of nonstandard Spanish orthography in Spanish classes. Thus many Latinos/as, those who traveled to the center from the periphery, are constantly serving as cultural translators. As cultural translators, they are translated by their use of Spanish. They also encounter other translated people and

---

17. Stavans, *Spanglish*, 177–78. My mother used to write me notes in Spanish, but when using the verb *estoy* (first-person singular), she would leave out the "s" and write *etoy*. To see studies on the variations of Puerto Rican Spanish, see Miquel Simonet, Marcos Rohena-Madrazo, and Mercedes Paz, "Preliminary Evidence for Incomplete Neutralization of Coda Liquids in Puerto Rican Spanish," in *Selected Proceedings of the Third Conference on Laboratory Approaches to Spanish Phonology*, ed. Laura Colantoni and Jeffrey Steele (Somerville, MA: Cascadilla Proceedings Project, 2008), 72–86; see also Marcos Rohena-Madrazo, "Superlative Movement in Puerto Rican Spanish and General Spanish," *NYU Working Papers in Linguistics* 1 (2007): 1–31.

translate their own home experiences to each other to form new languages such as Spanglish.

How does all of this relate to translating the Lord's Prayer? Not directly; rather, the Lord's Prayer, as text, calls attention to the issues of language, translation, and interpretation of the reader himself or herself (themselves) as well as the text itself. It does so because, like any text that is of another world and time, it sparks a desire to understand. The language and translation of the Lord's Prayer evoke questions about what happens when translation occurs (crosses over) and how it changes the translator as well as the text. Thus, as previously discussed, language, translation, and interpretation are intertwined workings in culture. Translation of language is not simply a one-way process. It is a two-way process in which I translate the text and the text translates me, thus producing an interpretation for each. It is a cultural interaction and at times an act of reempowerment via agency. This activity of translation—bringing the text into dialogue with Latino/a identity—is one I aim to explore within a dialogical approach. The purpose of this particular engagement of the Lord's Prayer is to investigate this exploration. Thus, what follows is a literary analysis of the Lord's Prayer through the optic of language, translation, and interpretation, shedding light on the prayer's overall strategy to struggle against conformity as a way to live.

Analysis of the Text

Given this background on language, translation, and interpretation from a Latino/a optic, how would such a background play a role when brought to bear on the Lord's Prayer in Matthew (6:9b–13)? In this second part, I shall explore briefly the literary identity (structuration and syntax) of the Lord's Prayer, followed by a modest discussion of the effect of a Latino/a optic on the identity of the document.[18]

---

18. For an example of the dialogical approach from an ecological hermeneutical perspective, see Vicky Balabanski, "An Earth Bible Reading of the Lord's Prayer: Matthew 6.9–13," in *Readings from the Perspective of the Earth*, ed. Norman C. Habel, Earth Bible 1 (Sheffield: Sheffield Academic, 2000), 151–61.

Lord's Prayer (6:9b–13) as a Literary Text

Matthew's Lord's Prayer (6:9b–13) is found in the narrative unit of the Sermon on the Mount (5:1–7:27), in which Jesus is portrayed as a teacher who is revealing the identity of God. The Sermon on the Mount is the first of five major discourses in Matthew (5:1–7:27; 10:5–42; 13:1–52; 18:1–35; and 24:3–25:46)—all of which may be organized around community-related themes, including the Sermon on the Mount (5:1–7:27).[19]

The Lord's Prayer falls within the narrative section of the sermon involving "The Teaching of Jesus" (6:1–18). The prayer proper (6:9b–13) follows two subsections, "Instruction on Almsgiving" (6:1–4) and "Teaching about Prayer" (6:5–9a), and two subsections follow the prayer proper, "Instruction on Forgiveness" (6:14–15) and "Instruction on Fasting" (6:16–18), closing the entire narrative section itself (6:1–18). Overall, all four subsections (6:1–4; 6:5–9a; 6:14–15; 6:16–18) surrounding the prayer (6:9b–13) involve the Matthean Jesus providing instruction to the disciples (broadly understood) on how to practice their piety (almsgiving, praying, and fasting) in the spirit of true worship of God, unlike the "hypocrites" (*hypokritai*)[20] in the synagogue. Thus the relationship between these subsections and the prayer itself suggests that the Lord's Prayer serves as a central division (6:9b–13) within the central narrative section (6:1–18), functioning in a didactic and apologetic fashion and framed as a petition or direct response to God.

Focusing on the prayer proper (6:9b–13), six petitions (6:9c, 10a, 10b, 11, 12a, 13b) are contained within the prayer on how to pray to God: "Our Father in heaven" (*pater hēmōn ho en tois ouranois* [6:9b]). Prior to the prayer proper, the prayer begins with a direct, though polite, command (9a) through the use of a present imperative by the Matthean Jesus to the target readers on how to pray and how to continue praying: "You then pray like this" (*houtōs oun proseuchesthe hymeis* [6:9a]). This

---

19. Here I am following Benjamin W. Bacon's structuration of Matthew simply as a heuristic tool; see Bacon, *Studies in Matthew* (London: Constable, 1930). An alternative and simpler outline, governed by a christological reading, can be found in Jack Dean Kingbury, *Matthew: Structure, Christology, Kingdom* (Philadelphia: Fortress, 1975); Kingbury, *Matthew as Story* (Philadelphia: Fortress, 1988).

20. All translations in the remainder of the volume are my own unless otherwise indicated.

particular text (6:9a) is not part of the prayer proper, but it draws the reader away from the sphere of the earthly/imperial realm and into the sphere of God/imperial realm that follows (6:9b). The use of this imperative ("pray" [*proseuchesthe*]) by the Matthean Jesus (6:9a), therefore, constructs two communities: a narrative community that prays incorrectly and falsely ("hypocrites") and within the world of the public eye, and a new community that prays correctly and truthfully (disciples) and within the world of God (reign of God in the present).[21] Thus the world is spatially dualistic.

Such a clear either/or construction of the world may not resonate with many Latinos/as, including myself, who find themselves uncomfortable with having to choose only one way to pray or one language (English) to worship in, for that matter. Once a dualistic or an either/or framework is established, it can compel many to conform to or choose one world over another and associate the "outsider" with the "hypocrite" and the "insider" with the "true" believer. My cultural experience with language and translation suggests that when this type of dichotomous choice is presented as the only option, hierarchies are established, consciously or unconsciously, as with languages. These hierarchies are analogous to the issue of superior/inferior dialects in Spanish and English mentioned above. Moreover, the prayer itself is introduced around an either/or world when it calls for a proper way to say a prayer. A Latino/a experience may challenge this either/or world as it does when challenging laws that force them to choose between languages. Yet, on the other hand, to be fair, many Latinos/as may receive this either/or construct well, especially in establishing their identity as "insiders" in the United States by calling for the learning of English as the gateway to the "American Dream"—as I once did.[22] Thus, the delimitation of the constitutive subsections surrounding the prayer contributes to an ideological binary narrative world.

---

21. See also Kingsbury, *Matthew as Story*, 130. See also the pathbreaking volume by Warren Carter, *Matthew and Empire: Initial Explorations* (Harrisburg, PA: Trinity Press International, 2001), who reads Matthew as a counternarrative to the Roman imperial system.

22. Stavans, *Spanglish*, 3.

Narrative Analysis

As indicated above, the Lord's Prayer in Matthew begins with a call to the Father, "Our Father in heaven."[23] This call indicates three key items. First, the Father belongs to everyone. This is supported by the genitive plural personal pronoun "our" (*hēmōn*), thus establishing a universal understanding of God. Second, God is addressed as the "Father" (*pater*), thus constructing a world governed solely by a male character and, consequently, envisioned solely from a monotheistic perspective. Finally, the spatial location of the Father is "in heaven" (*en tois ouranois*), thus constructing a location where the "Father" exists as well as representing a hierarchical world—the world of heaven to come—that is superior to the current hypocritical world.[24]

From the perspective of a Latino/a optic on language, translation, and interpretation, the question of hierarchy finds expression again in this call to prayer. The fundamental issue of this call is how the notions of mother and father are placed in opposition and, thus, in a hierarchy. In language, the use of proper or Castilian Spanish or New England English has become associated with elite membership and power (insiders and outsiders), and those who do not speak in these normative dialects are identified (by some) as less powerful Others. Likewise, in this text, the term Father became associated with the notion that men should be in higher positions than women and ultimately evolved into the notion that power was the sole property of men.[25] This notion translated as patriarchy—not to mention the formation of a particular view of masculinity—still remains strong among many Latino/a communities, as evidenced through the voices of Latinas.[26] The language of Father thus creates tension in a world where

---

23. Eugene M. Boring, "The Gospel of Matthew: Introduction, Commentary and Reflection," *NIB* 8:89–505.

24. Ibid.

25. I do understand that for many Latinos/as and others, the metaphor of Father (Padre) has enduring and comforting symbolism, particularly in times of need. I am not trying to take away this sense of connection, but rather I am suggesting that for others it may mean something different.

26. See Isasi-Díaz, *Mujerista Theology*; Elsa Tamez, *Against Machismo* (Yorktown Heights, NY: Meyer-Stone, 1987).

Latinas remain hidden from view in many ecclesiastical and cultural leadership roles.

Six petitions to the Father follow this brief call to God. The first three petitions (6:9c, 10a, 10b), with the force of a request, are politely directed toward God and supported by the second-person singular genitive pronoun "your" (*sou*) in all three petitions. In the first petition, "Hallowed be your name" (6:9c), the imperative "hallowed" or "make holy" (*hagiasthētō*) conveys the force of a pronouncement or statement requesting that God's name be honored. This subtle petition provides reverence to God by calling on the reader to worship or venerate God by respecting his name. In other words, the Matthean Jesus, who is in authority, is beseeching the petitioner to submit to a superior God. The second petition (6:10a), also beginning with an imperative and with the force of a statement, "your kingdom come [*elthetō*]," calls for the reign or kingdom (*basileia*) of God to be present in the here and now. Thus bringing the reign of God to the present world means establishing God's rule (empire) now and not later.[27] Finally, the third petition (6:10b), initiated with another pronouncing imperative, "be done" (or "be made" or "be created" [*genēthētō*]), calls for the will of God to be completed as well ("your will be done" [*genēthētō to thelēma sou*]).[28] This call brings forth God's intentions and reign upon those who are not righteous in this world. In other words, it is a petition to bring into this world what is already present in heaven ("on earth as it is in heaven"), accentuated with the particle of comparison "as" (*hōs* [6:10c]). These first three requests/petitions initiate the reign and will of God in the here and now and accentuate a world ruled by God, thus overturning or abolishing a world governed by "hypocrites." In short, it is a call for one world to prevail over another in the name of the Father—a world (patriarchal, monotheistic) of conformity where all other religions or systems are placed in a most perilous situation.

In commending this particular call, the prayer leaves no room for negotiation on how to pray and what to pray for: the reign of God in the here and now is the appeal. For many Latinos/as, where one uses Spanish—whether it is inside or outside the home or both—is a matter of frequent discussion and debate. Interestingly, for some members of

---

27. See Carter, *Matthew and Empire*, 9–19. See also *NIB* 8:203.

28. This text (6:10b) is missing in Luke's version of the prayer (Luke 11:2–4).

the older generations (first-generation and 1.5-generation folks), the use of any Spanish was seen as impeding the assimilation experience in the United States. The truth is that parents and grandparents, including my own, insisted (as in the use of the imperative) that children speak English as a way to improve the family's economic condition. The result, however, is the unconscious denial of one's cultural heritage. Similarly, the Matthean Jesus calls for a better condition of the world via the reign of God and demands acceptance of the "right" way to pray, not realizing that such an imperative command comes with ramifications—a sense of conformity for all outsiders.

The second set of petitions (6:11, 12, 13) refers to humans and is also cast in the imperative (6:11, 12a, 13b)—except for two verbs in the aorist (6:12b, 13a)—which conveys a summary command, with the second verb ("do not bring" [mē eisenegkēs]) supported by the negative particle mē (6:13a). These petitions all make requests on behalf of human beings, as opposed to requesting things that pertain to God, as witnessed in the first three petitions. This is easily supported through the use of first-person plural pronouns—"us" (hēmin), "our" (hēmōn), and "we" (hēmeis)—that returns the attention to humanity.

The beginning of this second set of petitions is the fourth petition, "Give us this day our daily bread" (6:11). The word "give" (dos) is again in the imperative, but this time softened to suggest a request rather than a demand.[29] But I read it slightly differently, with a force of urgency and specificity.[30] This urgent request is on behalf of "us" (hēmin), the ones appealing. It is a request for all those who are not included among those who are hypocrites from the point of view of the narrative unit. It is a request that is not for tomorrow but for the present, as supported by the adverb sēmeron ("today" or "this day"). The request is for bread (arton), which actually begins the clause in Greek, thus suggesting its centrality and importance in the petition. It is bread that signifies or calls attention to issues of hunger and nourishment as well as poverty.[31] The adverb

29. James A. Brooks and Carlton L. Winbery, Syntax of New Testament Greek (Lanham, MD: University Press of America, 1979), 128.

30. See Daniel B. Wallace, Greek Grammar: Beyond the Basics (Grand Rapids: Zondervan, 1996), 720.

31. NIB 8:204. See also Ivoni Richter Reimer, "The Forgiveness of Debts in Matthew and Luke: For an Economy without Exclusions," in God's Economy: Bibli-

"daily" (*sēmeron*), modifying "give," points to the frequency of receiving this bread. This is bread not just for today but also for tomorrow.[32] The call for bread as the first request on behalf of a community, therefore, points to the claim that bread signifies nourishment for a community that is hungry, poor, and simply trying to survive the consequences of existing as Others within the confines of an empire.[33]

From the Latino/a optic discussed above, speaking neither Spanish nor English properly is a signifier of less education and poverty. How one speaks and what one eats are often associated with where one is located. Often, poverty, hunger, and lower levels of education are associated with lower socioeconomic classes where these factors are daily realities of survival. They are also realities of power in empires that neglect or are merciless towards the poor. That the prayer mentions bread as one of its requests thus signals an expression of the lower classes among its narrative hearers. This petition, therefore, underscores the contrast between the world of the powerful and the world of the powerless that presently shapes human existence in the narrative world.

The fifth petition (6:12) of the Lord's Prayer consists of two clauses: "And forgive us our debts, as we also have forgiven our debtors" (*kai aphes hēmin ta opheilēmata hēmōn, hōs kai hēmeis aphēkamen tois opheiletais hēmōn* [6:12a, 12b]). The independent clause (6:12a) makes a request on behalf of the community once again, and the dependent adverbial clause (6:12b) draws a comparison or analogy that indicates how forgiving ought to be done. What is more, the petition begins with a transitional conjunction, "and" (*kai*), continuing the pattern of requests already made in the Lord's Prayer. What follows is an imperative of entreaty using of the word "forgive" (*aphes*), thus calling for a softening of the request and perhaps suggesting that the word "please" accompanies the imperative ("please forgive").[34] Again, the request is on behalf of a community, as expressed through the use of the pronouns "us" (*hēmin*) and "our" (*hēmōn*). The object of the petition is "debts" (*opheiletais*). Whereas the previous object

---

cal Studies from Latin America, ed. Ross Kinsler and Gloria Kinsler (Maryknoll, NY: Orbis Books, 2005), 152–68.

32. Reimer, "Forgiveness of Debts."
33. See Carter, *Matthew and Empire*, 9–19.
34. Brooks and Winbery, *Syntax of New Testament Greek*, 128.

of request was "bread" (*arton*), signifying poverty and nourishment, here the word "debt" surely implies an economic reality.[35]

One of the identity markers from the optic of language and translation is the question of origins. How one uses a particular word, whether it is in English or Spanish, leads one to draw conclusions the origins of words and identity. Similarly, one of the major issues regarding the Lord's Prayer is how to translate the Greek words *opheilēmata/tois opheiletais* ("debts"/"debtors" or "trespass"/"those who trespass"). As in any translation, a betrayal of the "original" exists.[36] As such, the quest for the original meaning and context is an aim for translators. This quest necessarily leads readers in the English-speaking world to decide which translation to use in Matthew's prayer. Does one use "debts/debtors" or "trespass/those who trespass"—the two dominant English variations of the Greek? It is the former that has prevailed in many English translations.[37] My point here is not to challenge the prevailing translation of Matt 6:12 and thus argue for one different from the standard "debts/debtors." Rather, my intention is to call awareness to the activity of translation in order to show that language, translation, and interpretation are not only inaccurate activities, in the sense that one is always interpreting when translating language, but also to demonstrate that language and translation of ancient and modern texts always involves some sort of reflection on origins and explanation of identity. The problem is that this quest for origins, the desire to arrive at the intended meaning, is more about the person translating and interpreting the history of the word than it is about capturing the word's original meaning.[38] The quest for origins views the text as static with an original intent—something to retrieve.

---

35. See Reimer, "Forgiveness of Debts," 152–68.

36. The notion of "original" is problematic.

37. E.g., "And forgive us our debts, as we also have forgiven our debtors" (ASV, NASB, NIV, RSV, NRSV); "And forgive us our debts, as we forgive our debtors" (NAB). In Spanish: "Como también nosotros perdonamos a los que nos ofenden" (Sagrada Biblia); "Y perdónanos nuestras deudas, como también nosotros hemos perdonado a nuestros deudores" (La Biblia de las Américas); "Perdónanos nuestras deudas, como también nosotros hemos perdonado a nuestros deudores" (La Nueva Internacional).

38. See Thiselton, *Hermeneutics*, 26. Thiselton is actually making reference to James Barr's work on semiotics, *The Semantics of Biblical Language* (Oxford: Oxford University Press, 1961), 107–60, see esp. n. 21. Barr was referring to the history of words as opposed to the person translating (my point).

For instance, the translation of *opheilēmata/tois opheiletais* as "debts" and "debtors" has its roots in the King James Version (KJV)[39] of the Bible of 1611, which drew its translations from the words *debita* and *debitoribus* in the Latin Vulgate.[40] As readers have learned from Sugirtharajah's work on the KJV's reception history, these translations are part of the colonial enterprise of the British culture and empire. The British Empire imposed this translation upon its colonies, and the KJV translation ultimately became the standard. Other very important English-speaking translators such as William Tyndale (1526) preferred "trespass" and "trespassers" ("And forgeve vs oure treaspases even as we forgeve oure trespacers"), yet Myles Coverdale (1535) in his translation of the prayer translates the Greek words as "debts" and "debtors" ("And forgeue vs oure dettes, as we also forgeue oure deters"). John Wycliffe in 1395 ("And foryyue to vs oure dettis, as we foryyuen to oure dettouris") makes the same translation choice of "debts" and "debtors."

Clearly, the translation of Matthew's Lord's Prayer has varied throughout history, but the dominant tradition has been to translate *opheilēmata/ tois opheiletais* into English as "debts" and "debtors." Both are possible translations of the ancient Greek terms *opheilēmata/tois opheiletais*. However, by the fourteenth century, English translators, turned to second- and third- century Latin translations of the Christian Bible and rendered the Latin terms *debita* and *debitoribus* in the Lord's Prayer with two English terms that looked quite similar—"debts" and "debtors." Similarly, the Latin Catholic Mass, which bases the Lord's Prayer on Matthew's version, reads: "*Et dimitte nobis debita nostra, sicut et nos dimittimus debitoribus.*" In English, this reads: "And forgive us our trespasses, as we forgive those who trespass against us."[41] From this brief discussion, one can observe that language, translation, and interpretation are never purely dynamic (idea for word) or literal (word for word).[42] Like the history of *opheilēmata/*

---

39. "And forgiue vs our debts, as we forgiue our debters" (KJV).

40. "*Et dimitte nobis debita nostra sicut et nos dimisimus debitoribus nostris*" (Matt 6:12 Vulg.).

41. *Latin-English Booklet Missal for Praying the Traditional Mass*, 4th ed. (Glenview, IL: Coalition in Support of *Ecclesia Dei*, 2009), 38–39.

42. See George Aichele, "The Translator's Dilemma: A Response to Boer, Coker, Elliott, and Nadella," in Elliot and Boer, *Ideology, Culture, and Translation*, 59–65.

tois opheiletais, translating and interpreting the identities of Latinos/as is a constructive enterprise, saying more about the history of Latinos/as and those doing the construction than about a universal picture of them.

The sixth petition consists of two clauses. The first independent clause (6:13a) contains the first and only negative petition in the Lord's Prayer. This petition begins with the transitional conjunction "and" (*kai*), continuing the flow of requests already present in the Lord's Prayer. The independent clause, "And do not lead us into temptation" (*kai mē eisenenkēs hēmas eis peirasmon*), is placed in the subjunctive mood, as expressed through the plea "do not lead" (*mē eisenenkēs*), thus calling for a prohibition of leading the community ("us" [*hēmas*]) "into temptation" (*eis peirasmon*).

The second dependent clause (6:13b) concludes the final petition of the Lord's Prayer. It begins with the contrastive, emphatic conjunction "but" (*alla*); thus the petition pivots to a different request from the one it is subordinate to, namely, "Do not lead us into temptation" (6:13a). Returning to the imperative mood, as expressed through the verb "deliver" (*rhusai*), the petition asks God to "rescue" the community from "the evil one" (*tou ponērou*) or "evil" in the general sense, as some translations have suggested. This time the request is not for nourishment or economic forgiveness but deliverance from the evil temptations (the systematic immorality) that surround the community. The petition calls for the reader/hearer to reflect on the life lived in the world of the Father (6:9b).

The sixth petition depicts an evil world. From the Latino/a optic discussed above, language, translation, and interpretation may lead to a deliverance from the sort of evil world encompassed by an either/ or dichotomous sense of language. Depending on one's stance regarding the use of English and/or Spanish (and their particularities) as part of a Latino/a identity, one might find coming to terms with the constant mutation of language, translation, and identity as a kind of deliverance. Not deliverance in the theological sense, but rather deliverance in the sense of living between languages and translations. The "evil one" is the one that aims to teach a particular model of language as the only way, with the intent to civilize. I suspect this includes even those who teach and advocate a single "right" method of prayer and worship.

Conclusion

As I initially stated, this discussion is intended to be more illustrative or didactic than definitive. In other words, my initial examination of the Lord's Prayer through the question of language, translation, and interpretation is meant to provide a sample of Latino/a hermeneutics that aims to bring attention to the dialogical approach—as I see it. It not only highlights issues related to language, translation, and interpretation within the Latino/a community, but also brings this into dialogue with the prayer's identity through language, translation, and interpretation. At the same time, the prayer itself, through its six petitions, captures some concerns that reflect realities in the Latino/a and other communities. For instance, as the first set of petitions suggests, the (spatial) world is often cast in dualistic terms with the goal that the reader should conform to one or the other (world above, world below). Yet the second set of petitions calls attention to the earthly, living realities of bread, debt, and evil that many people experience in the here and now, thus revealing another dualistic world separating privilege from poverty. This prayer captures well the realities that many Latinos/as experience on a daily basis—living in a dualistic world and having to conform to various either/or binary situations such as language. At the same time, the prayer petitions God in order to resist such dualistic spatial worlds on earth here and now as it will be done in the future. I follow the latter reading, understanding this prayer's petition to God as a strategy for resisting this either/or binary.

A dialogical approach can take many directions but it does not aim to provide affirmation of a text's intent as visible in many modernist approaches and methods, nor does it aim to equate the lived experience of Latinos/as with the lived experienced projected by either the historical audience or literary audience of a text as the strategy of correlation does. Rather, the dialogical approach aims to employ the text as a (constructed) conversation partner, thus allowing the text's language, translation, and interpretation and the reader's Latino/a experience with language, translation, and interpretation an opportunity to hear one another. A conversation or dialogue cannot take place unless both partners (text and reader) are speaking about the same issue. It is a constructed conversation that takes place between the text and the reader. It is in this between space where meaning is located.

5

Galatians 2:11–14: An Ideological Strategy

In the previous chapters, representative readings from a correlation strategy and a dialogical strategy illustrated the approach of various Latino/a biblical scholars. As I mentioned in the first chapter, not all Latino/a biblical scholars read texts using these strategies, but many draw aspects from one or both of them. In fact, seldom is one approach used exclusively. In this final chapter, I will use a third reading strategy that is also rarely used entirely alone—the ideological strategy.

An ideological reading of text also sees the text as a conversation partner, but it works with the assumption that the text and the reader are infused with an ideological discourse that takes form in the set of beliefs or values by which society (or individuals) creates a certain kind of world—historical or literary. Hence, both text and reader are constructions exerting influence on the world around. These ideological readings aim to expose oppressive systems of meaning in texts (e.g., racialization, colonialism, patriarchy) that have been selected, crafted, imagined, and arranged with a particular purpose and/or highlight liberative or ambiguous systems of meaning in texts (e.g., egalitarianism, freedom, justice). In a sense, all Latino/a biblical readings are ideological, but the focus on ideology in this particular approach is heightened. What is more, ideology forms us as readers. We are also informed by systems of meaning emanating from texts and communities. The way we speak about our identities or ourselves (e.g., Latino/a) functions to promote an ideology—for better or for worse. Finally, even interpretations are ideological and produce a system of meaning that must undergo an ethical-critical evaluation. For these reasons, the text, reader, and interpretations are inherently ideological. An ideological strategy purposely challenges any uncritical reading that accepts the world created for readers by the powerful.[1]

Consequently, whereas a correlation approach aims to establish a linear relationship between reader and text, and a dialogical approach aims to establish a conversation on a particular topic or theme between reader and text, an ideological approach aims to establish a conversation in which the systems of meaning between reader and text are highlighted and evaluated with the purpose of proposing an alternative worldview or ideology from its interpretation. I would position my particular strategy of reading in line with this ideological strategy, as reflected below. In this way, a Latino/a ideological reading is equal to other ideological readings of texts yet distinct in that it brings to bear a topic reflected in many Latino/a communities.

Introduction

A perennial question for established communities is the question of how to receive new ethnic/racial minorities to the United States. It does not have to pertain only to questions of migration; it could also apply to gender and sexuality or religious or class identities, to name a few. For instance, if one takes a look at the Latino/a community, Latinos/as are often racialized subjects and perceived as newcomers, even though many have been in the United States even before the United States became the United States. Such misconceptions often lead to the characterization of all Latinos/as as migrants, thus generating demands for controlling the flow of migration, securing the border between Mexico and the United States, and/or tightening the labor market so Latinos/as do not take jobs away from native-born workers, that is, white US Americans. Seldom do established communities focus their discussion on how best to incorporate migrants or the Other as part of a community. It is often a discussion of how Latinos/as ought to

---

1. The tools employed with this strategy are varied. They may include various forms of historical and literary reconstructions informed by all sorts of ideological orientations—e.g., feminist, imperial, postcolonial, or liberation—applied to texts and readers. All such tools are also imbued with ideology, so such tools and orientations must also be subjected to a metacritique or a theorization of their respective assumptions.

be excluded or totally assimilated. Such realities are not unique to Latinos/
as and can be witnessed among many marginalized communities at the
macro as well as micro levels. Such realities have led me to explore other
related questions, such as understanding the consequences of inclusion
and exclusion in relation to recognition and hospitality.

How a receiving community recognizes or values the differences (via
representation, interpretation, and communication)[2] of newly arrived
ethnic/racial migrants influences how the newly arrived ethnic/racial
migrants will be received. The challenge, I suspect, that many communities face today—as in the future—is how to facilitate the integration of
ethnic/racial minoritized groups into the receiving community (or nation)
and how these groups can incorporate themselves into the receiving communities. This reciprocal act begins with recognition and hospitality on
the part of both the receiving community (host) and the arrivant (guest).[3]

Both the ideas of recognition and hospitality are understood differently across time and space. Recognition, for this chapter's purposes,
concerns the struggles of identity—namely, national origins, gender,
sexuality, ethnicity, or race—and the value these social factors have as a
way to be rendered ethnic/racial communities visible and part of existing
dominant communities.[4] Recognition calls for a reciprocal act between
host and guest, where one subject recognizes the other and vice versa, as
a way of constituting subjectivity.[5] In other words, one is seen in relation
to another both as equal and as different. Recognition espouses sameness
and difference at the same time. Connected to recognition is hospitality.
Hospitality, depending on whether or not another is recognized, calls for
the reciprocal act of generosity, which takes on many expressions. For
hospitality to function in a perfect fashion, generosity must be expressed
reciprocally between host and guest—the two traditional figures in the
act of hospitality. Thus both recognition and hospitality are ideal notions,

---

2. See Nancy Fraser and Axel Honneth, "Introduction: Redistribution or Rec-
ognition," in *Redistribution or Recognition? A Political-Philosophical Exchange*, ed.
Nancy Fraser and Axel Honneth, trans. Joel Golb, James Ingram, and Christiane
Wilke (London: Verso, 2003), 13.

3. See Jacques Derrida, *Of Hospitality*, trans. Rachel Bowlby (Stanford, CA:
Stanford University Press, 2000).

4. See Fraser and Honneth, "Introduction," 13.

5. Ibid., 10.

yet often both notions are difficult (or nearly impossible) to reach in a sustained fashion because of a lack of trust or partial trust between the host and guest due to a variety of issues that are in one way or another connected to power.[6]

In this final chapter, I aim to explore these notions (recognition and hospitality) by examining how they play out in Galatians, particularly 2:11–14—the table meal scene in Antioch. The table meal represents a traditional spot where recognition and hospitality operate.[7] The meal is an important venue where recognizing the equal value of another and expressing generosity are practiced. It is not the only spot where recognition and hospitality appear in ancient literature, but it is a representative place where there is typically a host and a guest with textual expressions of recognition and hospitality at play.[8] Thus, both these notions are brought to bear on Galatians and, in particular, to the table meal in 2:11–14.

To support this reading, first, I will focus on the occasion of the letter in relationship to recognition and hospitality. Examining the relationship between 2:11–14 and the rest of the letter helps us to place 2:11–14 within the letter's design and development. Second, I discuss recognition and hospitality in general in Galatians. Third, I explore the values of recognition and hospitality in selected passages in Galatians in order to show that these ideas undergird the letter, including 2:11–14. Fourth, I perform a close ideological reading of 2:11–14 to illustrate how recognition and hospitality are played out in one particular text. Finally, I reflect critically on the question of recognition and hospitality today.

---

6. Derrida would argue that hospitality is not so much an object to know as an experience that is in constant tension. See Derrida, *Of Hospitality*.

7. See John Koenig, *New Testament Hospitality: Partnerships with Strangers as Promise and Mission*, OBT 17 (Philadelphia: Fortress, 1985), 68.

8. See Andrew Arterbury, *Entertaining Angels: Early Christian Hospitality in its Mediterranean Setting*, NTM 8 (Sheffield: Sheffield Phoenix, 2005). Arterbury argues for a narrow understanding of hospitality referring to strangers or travelers who receive provisions or protection from a host. This core understanding of hospitality functions across texts and time. This particular reading or recovery of hospitality, informed by historical criticism, as it is traditional conceived and practiced, is done well. However, some might find his reconstruction of hospitality too narrow, thus constructing an illusion of totality. Nonetheless, the study is quite helpful in placing hospitality within a "constructed" historical and literary context.

I shall argue that both recognition and hospitality are ideal notions, yet they are also unstable depending on how the host and guests are influenced by whatever motives, customs, or interpretations of difference are functioning across time and space. In this ideological reading of 2:11–14, I read this text as an example of failed recognition and hospitality not because the guest (Cephas) "leaves" the table, so to speak, but rather because both the host and the guest fail to reciprocate recognition and hospitality. For both recognition and hospitality to operate, the host and the guest must both see each other as equals *and also* as respectfully different from one another. This ideal relation is at the core to establishing community; yet the tension involved in attaining it is challenging, as remains the case today when difference is incorporated into a community.[9]

Occasion: Recognition and Hospitality

From the point of view of Paul, as represented in my reading of Galatians, the occasion for the Letter to the Galatians is that Paul is concerned about outsiders who are disturbing or troubling (*hoi tarassontes* [1:7]) the minds of the Galatians (the named addressees [1:2]) and turning (*metastrepsai*) them away from the gospel of Christ and toward a different gospel contrary to Christ's gospel.[10] After Paul's last visit to the Galatian communities

---

9. The danger of reading this text as failed hospitality because the guest leaves the table is that one sees the host always as host and the guest always as guest. With such thinking, no one, especially the arrivant, will ever be fully recognized or welcomed (or deemed a member of that community) even though the community claims to recognize or welcome the arrivant as an equal.

10. Dunn argues that *hoi tarassontes* was used often to suggest political agitation (citing Acts 17:8, 13). Thus the negative connotation of the outsiders as "troublemakers" or "agitators" suggested by some translations of the word might be in keeping with Paul's meaning. However, these two translations lead English readers to conceptualize the outside group as opponents, thus influencing how they read the remainder of the letter. The word only appears in 1:7 in Galatians. Henceforth, knowing that all translations are value laden, I will employ the term *outsiders*. See James D. G. Dunn, *The Epistle to the Galatians*, Black's New Testament Commentary (Peabody, MA: Hendrickson, 1993), 43. The word *metastrepsai* appears in Paul's writings only here (Gal 1:7). From its usage elsewhere, J. Louis Martyn suggests it conveys the meaning "to alter something" or "to change

(1:6–9),[11] the Galatians changed their mind about what Paul had taught them ("you are so quickly [*tacheōs*] deserting" [1:6a]). Paul instructs the Galatians to remain committed to the gospel of Christ—the gift he delivered on behalf of God. In other words, in Paul's eyes, there is only one gospel (or interpretation) of Christ. At some point, a group—"some" (*tines* [1:7b])—came to the Galatians and preached another or different (*allo* [1:7a]) gospel contrary to the gospel of Christ. The very deliberative discourse (1:6–9) by Paul to the Galatians is an appeal for the Galatians to reject what these other teachers or outsiders are offering them.[12] Such rejection is a gesture of inhospitality.

Accordingly, the notion of hospitality is expressed throughout Galatians—either directly or indirectly. It is, according to Christine D. Pohl, what strongly defines a Christian in the first century.[13] One expression of hospitality, in the context of relationships with others, is the practice of mutual reciprocity, where two persons (or communities) welcome one another by exchanging hospitality. In other words, in this idealized notion of hospitality there exists a mutual blessing between parties.[14] This notion of hospitality is an example of an ethical expression of hospitality and one that is narrated often in ancient literature and the Scriptures, including

something to its opposite" (see Joel 2:31 LXX; Acts 2:20). See Martyn, *Galatians: A New Translation with Introduction and Commentary*, AB 33A (New York: Doubleday, 1997), 112. In agreement, Dunn also points to the strong desire by Paul to suggest that "the outsiders" aimed to change the gospel—for the better perhaps, from their point of view (*Epistle to the Galatians*, 43). On the topic of identity formation, see also Jeremy Punt, "'The Others' in Galatians," in Lozada and Carey, *Soundings in Cultural Criticism*, 45–54.

11. For Luke's recounting of Paul's visit to the region of Galatia, see Acts 16:1–6; 18:23.

12. Philip Esler also leans toward seeing much of Galatians in a deliberative format. See Esler, *Galatians*, New Testament Readings (London: Routledge, 1998), 59–61. The notion of hospitality may not always be direct or extended through overt gestures of generosity to strangers. Hospitality may not even be reduced to one particular understanding or employ the very word *xenia* itself. But its elements or characteristics, such as an openness to receive difference, are developments of the earlier understanding of hospitality as providing assistance to strangers. See Arterbury, *Entertaining Angels*, 6.

13. See Christine D. Pohl, *Making Room: Recovering Hospitality as a Christian Tradition* (Grand Rapids: Eerdmans, 1999), 15.

14. Ibid., 13.

Galatians. It is the recognition of difference and the practice of extending an invitation—traditionally to a stranger but also to others—to share a meal, shelter, or protection.[15] Also undergirding the occasion of the letter is the theme of recognition. Recognition is the entryway to this idealized or ethical notion of hospitality. Without recognition (respecting the stranger, the Other, or the known person), hospitality is difficult to practice in an ethical fashion. For instance, the occasion of this letter can be construed in terms of how one receives difference within a community. The two options can be imagined as opposite ends of a values continuum: Does one reject the outside group with their different gospel, or does one receive the outside group with their different ideas? This is surely a question that Paul evokes in his attempt to persuade the Galatians to repudiate a different gospel contrary to Christ's (or Paul's), for not to do so leads to a curse of exclusion (*anathema* [1:9c]) and thus a community contrary to God (1:8–9). If one cannot recognize the identity of these outsiders and respect their message, or vice versa, the result is exclusion, guided by fear and misfortune (*anathema*). What one has, from my position, is both sides vying for a redefinition of hospitality and recognition and wanting their definition to prevail. To be sure, such fear and negative portrayal of those with a different rhetoric or identity violates an ethical mode of hospitality that is based on complete and unconditional trust, respect, and recognition of the other. This fear of difference is perhaps closer to a mode of hospitality based on power and/or negotiation. The ideal of recognition, therefore, determines whether difference will be rendered visible or invisible, influencing how hospitality will be enacted or not (inhospitality).

Consequently, the occasion of the letter lends itself, among other possible readings, to an exploration of the ideas of recognition and hospitality. The very issues of what it means to value difference and whether or not to welcome difference speak to the ideas of recognition and hospitality. How these ideas are expressed will vary based on the words and actions of Paul, his guests, and Cephas (Peter) in 2:11–14.

---

15. Ibid., 4. See also Arterbury, *Entertaining Angels*, 6; Letty M. Russell, *Just Hospitality: God's Welcome in a World of Difference*, ed. J. Shannon Clarkson and Kate M. Ott (Louisville: Westminster John Knox, 2009), 1. Contrary to Arterbury, Russell takes a broader view of hospitality that brings contemporary issues to bear on the text.

Foregrounding Recognition and Hospitality

As mentioned above, recognition is a matter of valuing equity and human exchange and thus comes to expression through hospitality differently across time and space. The understanding of these ideas in the ancient world was not static and changed over time (even in antiquity) and was influenced by the contexts in which the writers operated at the time of narrative expression as well as by the readers who employed these texts.[16] A working principle in this study is that the ideas of recognition and hospitality can be brought to bear on the narrative world of Galatians, informed not only by historical understandings of recognition and hospitality but also by present-day understandings of recognition and hospitality. Meaning, if working with a postmodern notion of epistemology, is a dynamic process between the reader and the text—with a nod toward the reader in this ideological reading of 2:11–14. Thus the historical world (constructed with a reader) out of which these ideas (recognition and hospitality) emerged is important to keep in mind out of respect to the identity of the text, but just as important is the cultural expression within the narrative world (constructed with a reader). One is not more important than another; at this time, I am simply more interested in the latter, the cultural expression reflected in the text (its texture and expression) and its effect as a literary and ideological product.

What is more, when and where recognition and hospitality are employed will vary from culture to culture.[17] It can also be employed both

---

16. Arterbury's argument that there is a core understanding of hospitality that persists throughout ancient Mediterranean culture is based on the assumption that such reading is done objectively, as the original audience was intended to. What is more, his study works under the assumption that the recovery process is not shaped by the questions we asked. Rather it is done objectively. Both assumptions are not my assumptions in this chapter. While it is important to understand ideas within the context of their historical production, it is just as important to keep in mind that historical productions are constructions of the reader. Arterbury's reading is not a misreading; it is just one reading among numerous possible readings. Historical projects, I believe, also call for examination of what was imagined in light of what I (we) *think* might have happened. Thus, my reading of recognition and hospitality is simply an ideological construction of a text that brings to bear ideas of recognition and hospitality, keeping in mind that it is simply a partial reading. See Arterbury, *Entertaining Angels*, 8–11.

17. See Pohl, *Making Room*, 3–15. On the question of historiography, see

at the public and private levels of exchange by means of welcoming new arrivants into one's community or into one's home. Whereas most cases of recognition and hospitality involve the host and guest as strangers, the host and guest can even be friends. The activity that connects the host and guest is the practice of recognition. The hospitable encounter between the two figures happens if both the host and guest recognize one another as equal in worth. At the same time, beneath this recognition is the element of trust. Since hospitality comes with risks and failures, a degree of trust plays a role in various types of hospitalities. For example, in some instances of hospitality, such as in a *political* situation of seeking an agreement between countries or individuals, the hospitable act is based on partial trust, and thus host and guest only recognize each other conditionally. In a *colonial* situation, there is little or no trust among the figures of host and guest. The guests, thinking they are the hosts, make no real intent to recognize the real hosts.[18] In a more genuine or *ethical* hospitable situation, both the host and the guest have complete or open trust with one another and will not take advantage of one another. Both recognize each other. This general three-part analysis is simply a way to see the complexity behind recognition and hospitality and their various types of possible expressions. These expressions (political, colonial, and ethical), I believe, are reflected in the literary text as cultural expressions in places where recognition and hospitality are at play.[19]

Whether the hospitable relationships are based on a political, colonial, or ethical understanding of trust, all of the relationships between the figures of host and guest employ recognition as well. First, with the political notion of hospitality, where trust is simply partial, recognition is reciprocal yet conditional.[20] In other words, the host's and the guest's recognition of

---

Joyce Appleby, Lynn Hunt, and Margaret Jacob, *Telling the Truth about History* (New York: Norton, 1994).

18. The Romans' relationship of (not quite) "benevolent colonialism" with Palestine is a classic example discernible in Jewish and Christian writings.

19. The use of political, colonial, and ethical notions of hospitality emanates from the work of Richard Haswell and Janis Haswell, *Hospitality as Authoring: An Essay for the English Profession* (Boulder, CO: Utah State University Press, 2015), 16–30. I am employing their terms here heuristically as ways to understand hospitality. Their work is strongly informed by the theorist Derrida.

20. Ibid., 84–101.

one another is conditional and safeguarded by mutual obligation. As long as both figures are willing to give back quid pro quo or return an invitation to one's home, a partial recognition is at play. That is to say, the figures recognize each other on the condition that the agreements remain intact. This political mode of hospitality is present not only in today's world; it also shows glimpses of itself in the Jewish and Christian Scriptures.[21] Second, in the case of the colonial mode of hospitality, little or no trust is present where hospitality is at play, and, as a result, little or no recognition is possible. This mode of hospitality provides no guaranteed assurances to the parties; all agreements between the parties are regulated by or based on "house rules" and the recognition that both parties are suspicious of each other. This mode remains ever present across the globe, including in both the Jewish and Christian Scriptures.[22] Finally, the ideal mode of hospitality is the ethical mode. For this mode of hospitality to function perfectly, which it often does not, both parties need complete trust and openness to experiencing new relationships based on unconditional hospitality, and both parties, in effect, need to recognize with dignity and respect the other way of being.[23] Such an ethical mode of hospitality is what many aim to achieve today, with the best intentions, but it often entails risks and failures. It is a mode of hospitality governed by the "grand narrative" of the Jewish and Christian Scriptures, which commands that one welcome and recognize the Other or stranger, though this recognition is not always successful or is sometimes undermined by inhospitality—with violence—and nonrecognition.[24]

---

21. See, for instance, Rahab welcoming and protecting the stranger spies from the army of Joshua (Josh 2). See Amy C. Oden, ed., *And You Welcomed Me: A Sourcebook on Hospitality in Early Christianity* (Nashville: Abingdon, 2001), 17. In the New Testament, see 2 John 10–11 on the conditions of whom to invite into the community of believers.

22. Haswell and Haswell, *Hospitality as Authoring*, 84–101. For an example at the macro level, note the ancient Hebrews' presence as "outsiders" in Pharaoh's Egypt (Exod 2:8–22). In the New Testament, the occupation of ancient Palestine by the Romans comes to mind (Luke 2:1–3).

23. Ibid.

24. In the Hebrew Bible, the injunction to welcoming strangers (e.g., Gen 19; Exod 23:9; Lev 19:18, 34; 25:23; 1 Kgs 17–18) speaks to ethical hospitality as an important component of what it means to be "chosen." Ethical hospitality also serves as the "grand narrative" of the New Testament (e.g., Matt 25:31–46; Luke 14:12–14; Heb 13:2) to welcome the Other and stranger, for in welcoming them

For sure, recognition and hospitality are connected. The type of hospitality that is expressed influences how the parties recognize one another. The realities (modern or ancient) of the political or religious (to name a few) dimensions of the day redefine the type of hospitality and recognition delivered, as reflected in all three modes of hospitality above. I shall soon point out that this fluid understanding of recognition is also reflected in Galatians, particularly 2:11–14—the passage in question—where all three modes of hospitality are at play, characterized by various levels of trust, and leading to different experiences of recognition between Paul and Cephas and others. In what follows, a discussion of the theme of hospitality in Galatians will show that it is an indeed a strong expression throughout the letter.

Delimiting the Design of Galatians: Recognition and Hospitality

To help guide the reading of the theme of recognition and hospitality in Galatians, it is helpful to look first at the design of the Letter of Galatians. Demarcation of the outline, with an eye toward recognition and hospitality, provides a sense of the overall design of the letter. The general elements of rhetorical composition foreground this design.[25]

This letter begins with an introduction (1:1–11) that includes a salutation (1:1–5) typical of an ancient letter (prescript), followed by the occasion for the letter (1:6–11). The introduction lays the foundation for establishing Paul's authority in relation to others. In a sense, by reinforcing his authority, Paul reestablishes the border between the Galatians (and others) and himself, between his identity and that of the recipients (and others). He is willing to recognize all who believe in the gospel of Christ. By doing so, Paul embraces a notion of recognition and hospitality in which he casts himself as the host and the recipients as the guests,

---

one is helping Jesus. Both testaments point to the vision of a God who welcomes the marginalized (Pohl, *Making Room*, 16–35). The classic example of hospitality going wrong occurs when Lot offers his virgin daughters to the people of the town (Gen 19:8). On this latter point, see Pohl, *Making Room*, 26. In the New Testament, the household codes suggest, for example, how women ought to behave in order to be members of the community.

25. See George A. Kennedy, *New Testament Interpretation through Rhetorical Criticism*, SR (Chapel Hill: University of North Carolina Press, 1984).

forgetting that he came to the Galatians and not the other way around. He welcomes the Galatians to receive his own discourse and expects them to give back belief in reciprocation. The letter then moves towards a narrative that employs autobiography and history (1:12–24), thus reinforcing the recognition between Paul and the Galatians (and the other apostles). By drawing on autobiography and history, Paul takes the recipients (and modern readers) back to his past and to moments of hospitality and failed hospitality, as shall be seen in his narration of a meal in Antioch with Cephas and others (2:11–14). The letter then provides a summary of Paul's defense (2:15–21) and whether gentile believers will be recognized or excluded within the believing community for who they are and what they believe. Paul follows with arguments (3:1–6:10) that support his position established in 2:15–21. He uses the way one interprets a tradition such as the story of Abraham and Sarah (3:1–4:31) as well as how one ought to be living (or not) (the exhortation in 5:1–6:10) to reinforce his authority and role as host. The letter concludes (6:11–18) with Paul reestablishing or redrawing the boundaries of community by reinforcing his authority. Paul's "opponents" perhaps did not recognize that Paul is an authentic apostle of Christ, so Paul finishes his letter in his own writing (6:11), thus trying to convince the recipients to reject his opponents' (the outsiders') message and to welcome his message instead.

This demarcation of the design of the letter does not mention recognition or hospitality (*xenia*) directly, but there is surely an orientation that attends to Otherness, inclusion, exclusion, readiness to welcome, readiness to enter another world, and a readiness to participate in respecting difference. These are all aspects of recognition and hospitality that recast social relations.[26] To see moments of recognition and hospitality a bit closer in this letter, I will next briefly examine several texts.

Recognition and Hospitality: Galatians

As mentioned above, the themes of recognition and hospitality are not amply evident in Galatians, but both interrelated virtues are characteristically featured in several passages in the letter. But before I touch upon these passages, I shall first frame them with the context of ancient

---

26. See Oden, *And You Welcomed Me*, 14.

Hellenistic Christianity, which has its roots going far back to Homer's Odyssey and, of course, being informed by ancient Jewish Scriptures.[27] For recognition and hospitality are more clear and explicit in other ancient literature beyond Galatians. Ancient Hellenistic Christian hospitality, like modern hospitality, is based on the notion of generosity and goodwill between two parties or figures: host and guest. Where it differs is in its particulars—its practices, locations, and understandings. Andrew Arterbury argues that hospitality, for example, has a core that runs through time and space, which is also reflected in the New Testament. Ancient hospitality refers to strangers or travelers, and it is the act of helping travelers for a limited amount of time by way of provisions and protection.[28]

Recognition and hospitality across time and space do not always correlate with the present, argues Arterbury.[29] This is a valid point since values do change over time and are reflected in present cultural expressions, including expressions of recognition and hospitality. At the same time, though, the recovery of history is also socially located from the perspective of the one doing the reconstruction. Consequently, the recovery of recognition and hospitality in antiquity, for me, is a construction of recognition and hospitality informed by their historical production.[30] Hence, how recognition and hospitality are understood within various contexts (literary or social) shows their complex and varied usage. For instance, recognition and hospitality can be private (welcoming one to dinner) or public (welcoming one to a nation). They can involve receiving strangers or friends, exchanging gifts, or accompanying guests out of the community or city as a gesture of goodwill.[31] Yet undergirding recognition and hospitality is the age-old virtue of welcoming the stranger by way of food,

---

27. See Arterbury, "Part I: Mediterranean Hospitality in Antiquity," in *Entertaining Angels*, 15–132.

28. Ibid., 1–6.

29. Ibid., 1 n 1.

30. These expressions of recognition and hospitality appear in many places inside and outside of the New Testament, from the Pauline literature (Rom 14:1–15:7; 15:24; 16:23; 1 Cor 4:17; 16:6, 10–11, 17–34; 2 Cor 8:16–24; 11:8–9; Phil 1:5; 2:19–23; 4:10–20; Phlm 22; Heb 13:2) to the gospels (Matt 10:40; 11:28; 25:35–40; Mark 2:16; John 13:20; 14:2) to other literature of the period. For further texts, see Oden, *And You Welcomed Me*; Arterbury, *Entertaining Angels*.

31. See Arterbury, *Entertaining Angels*.

shelter, and protection no matter the identity of the person. All hospitality draws on some aspect of receiving the other, whether welcoming others, friends, or strangers with material things or simply welcoming them into the receiving community or society (as in today's world). As Thomas W. Ogletree says, recognition and hospitality call for a desire to need the Other beyond the fulfillment of one's wishes.[32] With this said, recognition and hospitality capture a wide range of possible meanings and actions.

The words used in the New Testament for hospitality are *xenia* and *philoxenia* (see Rom 12:13; Heb 13:2).[33] These terms suggest "the love of or attraction to hospitality."[34] Literally, *philoxenia* does not suggest a love of stranger from the noun *philo* (love) and *xenos* (stranger, host, or guest),[35] but rather, *philoxenia* denotes "a delight in the whole guest–host relationship." Put another way, the word stresses the relationship between host and guest and their deeply situated connection. Even the adjectival form *philoxenos* connotes the same meaning of relationship.[36] To witness and experience hospitality, therefore, is to enter into a committed relationship, either as host or guest, in which each participant reverses, or alternates between, the roles of host and guest. The host becomes guest, and the guest becomes host. This reversal is not easy to do—even with the best of intentions—and it sometimes creates tension and mistrust between the two parties. It can even create situations of direct inhospitality even when one is trying to teach or express hospitality (e.g., Mark 6:10–11; cf. Matt 10:11–15; Luke 10:5–12).[37] In fact, whether or not recognition and hospitality are ever successfully employed, one knows it is at play when there is tension between host and guest (as is the case in Gal 2:11–14).[38] In other words, recognition and hospitality percolate when both parties are

---

32. See Thomas W. Ogletree, *Hospitality to the Stranger: Dimensions of Moral Understanding* (Philadelphia: Fortress, 1985), 56–57.

33. See Arterbury, *Entertaining Angels*, 1; Koenig, *New Testament Hospitality*, 13 n. 7.

34. See Koenig, *New Testament Hospitality*, 13 n. 7.

35. Ibid., 8.

36. Ibid., 13 n. 7.

37. See Wayne A. Meeks, *The Origins of Christian Morality* (New Haven: Yale University Press, 1993), 106.

38. See Mireille Rosello, *Postcolonial Hospitality: The Immigrant as Guest* (Stanford, CA: Stanford University Press, 2001), 172.

making delicate decisions.[39] This uncomfortability keeps recognition and hospitality alive.[40] At the same time, one has to be cautious about romanticizing it. To take in a stranger (those outside and inside our notions of communities) or to bear gifts to a stranger comes with risk.[41] Sometimes the stranger stays too long in a house or place or at a table, which creates tension and makes the host behave unwelcomingly. As such, hospitality is not always easy to practice, but striving to practice it in order to establish relationships and know the other remains a goal. Hospitality became the means to establishing Christian partnership and community,[42] but in its quest to do so, it constructed identity and community with positive and negative consequences. The notion of recognition and hospitality served as a foundational construct that took root in early Christian writings and expanded into a variety of practices.[43] If we love God and God is in the stranger, then we must love the stranger[44]—this theological principle, as read in Judeo-Christian Scriptures, is not always practiced, as in the case with both Paul and Cephas in 2:11-14. Both figures lack trust in each other's relationship.

Galatians portrays how recognition and hospitality between Paul and the Galatians played out. As Arterbury illustrates, Paul did experience hospitality by the Galatians.[45] This would have been the case during his first visit (1:6a). Consequently, the Galatians recognized him through the reception of his message to them or his gift of the gospel to them. For instance, Arterbury points to Paul's reception by the Galatians when he was ill (4:13-14). The Galatians not only welcomed or received (*edechasthe*)[46] Paul during his first visit, they also recognized him as an angel of God—a divine messenger of God. This reception of Paul as an angel of God, according to Arterbury, mirrors Jewish hospitality, as when Abraham and other hosts welcomed incognito angels. What is more, the Galatians welcomed

---

39. Ibid., 172.
40. Ibid., 173.
41. Ibid., 172.
42. See Koenig, *New Testament Hospitality*, 40.
43. Ibid., 10.
44. Ibid., 4.
45. See Arterbury, *Entertaining Angels*, 102.
46. Ibid. Arterbury argues that *dechomai* ("to receive") is a word associated with hospitality.

Paul in a deserving fashion. Paul mentions that the Galatians received him "as Christ Jesus" (4:14c). In other words, employing the theological principle to welcome others as God would welcome them is in play with the Galatians and Paul.[47] Both Paul and the Galatians have a certain level of trust in one another—so it seems. The only condition of their relationship is that to be a member of the early Christian community, belief in the gospel of Christ is necessary. This condition moves recognition and hospitality closer to a political notion of hospitality.

Additional instances of recognition and hospitality can also be found in other locations in Galatians. For instance, an example of a passage that leans toward an ethical notion of hospitality is found in 5:14, when Paul introduces a command: "You shall love your neighbor as yourself." Paul's exhortation to the Galatians comes with a message on how to apply the Scriptures correctly (5:1–6:10). After persuading the Galatians that freedom does not mean succumbing to the spiritual elements of the world (4:8–10) or to circumcision or lack of circumcision (5:6a), but rather, freedom is achieved by "faith working through love" (*pistis di' agapēs energoumenē* [5:6b]), Paul exhorts the Galatians to use this freedom to be servants to one another (5:15c). Paul uses Scripture (drawing on Lev 19:18) to instruct the Galatians to love their neighbors as themselves. In fact, for Paul, the entire (whole) law is reduced to this one command. In this instance, Paul seems to be applying a more inclusive sense of hospitality. This ethical notion of hospitality fosters inclusion—to a certain extent! Again, Paul comes close to placing complete trust in the Galatians, but it is a trust partially safeguarded by the condition that the Galatians surrender themselves to Paul's exhortation. This "unconditional" notion of hospitality is not quite unconditional. It is unconditional only if the Galatians subscribe to Paul's understanding of freedom—a gospel over and against another gospel. This exclusive sense of hospitality is confirmed later when Paul finishes up his letter urging the Galatians to do good (*kairon*) to all people, and especially (*malista*) to those of the household of faith (6:10b–c). While open to a notion of an ethical hospitality for all, Paul qualifies this by calling for others to become like minded, for they will receive the gift that he bears (a gospel based on freedom as Paul's adherents see it). Though there is a glimpse of an ethical notion of

---

47. Ibid., 102.

hospitality where both parties have trust in each other, in the end, it is all on the condition of belief. Paul's extension of recognition and hospitality falls short once again.

An instance of inhospitality is also found in this argumentative section of Galatians (3:1–6:10). The retelling of the narrative of Hagar and the unnamed Sarah (4:21–31) seems to support a conditional notion of hospitality. Paul employs this text as a way to demonstrate how God ought to be served. The wives, Hagar and Sarah, and the birth of their sons, a slave and a free son, respectively, really point to an idea, an idea that suggests that one serves God either by relying on the promise (Christ) as Sarah did or by relying on the law, as Hagar did. The result is that Sarah's son is free and Hagar's son is a slave. Such an argument has implications for recognition and hospitality. Inscribed in this argument are the ideas of inclusion and exclusion. In the quest to suggest inclusion and acceptance of the other, recognition and hospitality paradoxically can be practiced in hostile ways as reflected in the narrative of Hagar and Sarah. The text of 4:21–31 is found at the beginning of a series of arguments (3:1–4:31) where Paul is making a defense for his gospel by proposing a particular reading of the Hagar and Sarah narrative found in the Hebrew Bible (Gen 21:10). By drawing upon this narrative, Paul at the end of the text argues to cast out Hagar and the son, for they are slaves. Such admonishment resonates not with recognition and hospitality but rather with nonrecognition and inhospitality. Even if he does not mean it so literally, Paul still suggests that the Galatians reject their way of life or the way they please God through the law. This notion of intended recognition and hospitality leads to nonrecognition and inhospitality and is based on very little trust or no trust whatsoever between believers and unbelievers. Also, in essence, Paul redraws the boundaries of the Christian community and thus redefines recognition and hospitality from one of inclusion toward one of exclusion.

These readings of recognition and hospitality in Galatians indicate that recognition and hospitality are at play in Paul's strategic argument. In a way, they all point toward recognition and hospitality as something bestowed toward "one's own kind" (believers only). Such a notion of recognition and hospitality to "one's own kind" is based on the exclusion of others because of their identity and/or way of life or belief. Paul in essence forgets (or not) that his authority as host or guest is strengthened through exclusion. When hospitality becomes a form of exclusion, the ideal or ethical notion of hospitality goes underground and reflects instances of colonial hospitality (when the guest becomes the host through power) or political hospitality (when agreements are based on fixed conditions).[48] Each of these narratives forces a rethinking of who is the host, who is the guest, and who has the power to define a notion of freedom, as Paul aims to do in Galatians. In what follows, by way of a literary reading of 2:11–14, we shall see an example of this in the way Paul and Cephas rethink their expectations of recognition and hospitality. In other words, what is more or less acceptable when difference confronts both of them?

Galatians 2:11–14: A Close Reading

Before providing an ideological reading of 2:11–14, a look at Paul's relations with the other disciples (2:1–10) provides some context for 2:11–14—the table meal incident in Antioch. Both passages deal with the theme of hospitality and recognition, although 2:11–14 is within the context of eating a meal, a common setting in the New Testament where hospitality and recognition are more obviously visible.[49] There is surely a link between these two passages (2:1–10 and 2:11–14), which are part of a larger narration (1:12–2:14) by Paul to establish the social arrangements in relation to the other apostles, thus reinforcing his authority.

The scene (2:1–10) begins in Jerusalem for Paul (and Barnabas and Titus). Titus is the gentile that Paul brings with him to demonstrate to the Jerusalem leaders that he indeed has authority from God to present the gospel of Christ to the uncircumcised (*to euangelion tēs akrobystias*), whereas Cephas, the Jerusalem leader, would present it to the circumcised (*tēs peritomes*). Both Paul and Cephas recognize each other with respect and equality in this passage (2:1–10). As a result, they both welcome each other into their spaces—spaces of their personal awareness and concern.[50]

---

48. Roji T. George surely brings questions of the colonial and hybridized context of Galatians to bear on his reading of the letter. See George, *Paul's Identity in Galatians: A Postcolonial Appraisal* (New Delhi, India: Christian World Imprints, 2016). Such a reading highlights the colonial relationship between Paul and the Galatians.

49. For example, see Mark 2:13–14; Luke 7:36–50; 15:1–2; 19:10.

50. See Koenig, *New Testament Hospitality*, 6.

In fact, the text of 2:9-10 makes mention of the practice of fellowship (*koinōnias*) as a gesture of hospitality, crowned with a handshake (2:9d). What is more, Paul's and Cephas's eagerness to help out the poor (2:10), which characterizes hospitality along with providing food, shelter, and protection to strangers, reinforces their partnership with one another (and with God) to serve as agents of God to the poor.[51] The resulting relationship of recognition and hospitality enables Paul and Cephas to welcome each other and respect each other on equal terms at the table in the following scene in Antioch.

Literary Context

Galatians 2:11-14 falls within the autobiographical and historical defense of Paul's letter (1:6-2:14). Prior to this line of argumentation, Paul makes it clear that his message or gospel did not come through humans but through God (1:1-5). This (Paul's) gospel is set against another gospel delivered to the Galatians and presented as the true gospel (1:6-10). The different understandings of these two gospels will be taken up later (2:15-21), but for now Paul defends his gospel by saying that it comes through God, as opposed to the outsiders' gospel, which comes through humans (1:10). Paul continues this argument by recounting his relations with the Jerusalem apostles (1:11-2:10). He first argues that his gospel did not come from the Jerusalem leaders (1:13-24) and then argues that when he delivered his gospel to the Galatians, the leaders added nothing to it (2:6). It is this rhetorical context that leads to the incident in Antioch that I wish to look at a bit closer in order to explore the theme of recognition and hospitality. It is the context of 2:11-14 that provides information regarding the issue or dispute between Paul and Cephas— that is, an internal Jewish "family" dispute on the meaning of recognition and hospitality.

Close Reading

The recounting of Paul's encounter with Cephas in Antioch (2:11-14) is centered on the ritual of a meal (*synesthien* [2:12]). The ancient meal

---

51. Ibid., 73.

signifies hospitality and thus serves as a ritual of acceptance.[52] It is at this meal that questions of recognition emerge and the roles of host and guest are established, held together at first by a level of trust. In 2:11–14, Paul and Cephas play out the dance of recognition and hospitality. Paul plays host while Cephas plays guest, for it is Cephas who comes to see Paul in Antioch (2:11). Although they begin by embracing one another as guest and host, they will end up on the opposite side of the table, so to speak. Although they begin on a continuum with the role of guest at one end and host at the other, this continuum will disappear by the end of the meal. In other words, the roles of guest and host will change. In what follows, I would like to explore how and why this continuum disappears, or, better, why recognition and hospitality gets redefined.

The passage in question can be examined according to an ABBA strucure for heuristic purposes. Both A components (2:11, 14) present a contrasting statement led by the adversative word "but" (*de* and *alla*), thus emphasizing the friction that led to a redefinition of a host–guest continuum. The B components (2:12, 13) both focus attention on the action of the guest (Cephas) that led to the friction. This picture of recognition and hospitality, therefore, challenges any ideal convention about recognition and hospitality, including the roles of guest and host.

Verse 11

Paul begins his recounting of the Antioch incident by briefing the reader/hearer on his position. In other words, Paul is not recounting this event without a situated position. He states immediately that the recognition and hospitality that was offered in 2:1–10 contained friction ("I opposed him") and that the guest was at fault for this friction ("he stood condemned" [*hoti kategnōsmenos ēn*]). As indicated, the recounting of the Antioch incident begins with the postpositive *de* ("but," "and"). The translation of this conjunction as "but" over the other possibility "and" suggests an adversative, indicating something contrary to what occurred before this event. In other words, the continuity of the sequence of events is disrupted at 2:11 with "but when" (*hote de*). From as early as 1:11, with his autobiographical sketch to support his defense as an apostle, Paul unfolds his story with the

---

52. See Dunn, *Epistle to the Galatians*, 117.

adverb "then" (*epeita* [1:18, 21; 2:1]), but when he gets to 2:11, the narrative looks back ("but when"), thus breaking the line of forward thinking.[53] Hence, the recounting of the incident at Antioch (2:11-14) begins with a contrastive statement, indicated by "but when" (*de hote*), pointing to some event that disrupted a moment of hospitality and recognition between Paul and Cephas as reflected in 2:1-10.

The temporal adverbial phrase "but when" in 2:11 introduces the moment when recognition and the act of hospitality bumps up against friction, along with other details of the setting: the location is Antioch, the principle figures are Paul and Cephas, and the resultant effect of this friction is that Cephas stood condemned (*hoti kategnōsmenos en*). Galatians 2:11 serves as a summary statement of the incident. First, the time of the incident is quite unclear. The adverb or particle *hote* ("when") puts the Antioch incident at some temporal location in the definite past before the "handshake" agreement with Peter (2:1-11) in historical time. But also, the particle (when), in relation to the principle verb ("opposed"), suggests that Cephas's arrival (*ēlthen*) is parallel with him opposing (*antestēn*) Cephas. Second, this look back also names Antioch as the site where this act of inhospitality takes place. Paul is recounting this incident through the location of Syrian Antioch, so to speak—with a Roman imperial background.[54] Third, the guest is Cephas, and since he is the one coming to Antioch to visit with Paul—Jerusalem being the home center for Cephas (2:1)—he is read as the guest in this scene. Consequently, Paul will serve as host.

Whether the letter is written from Antioch is hard to say, but it is a possibility.[55] What is known is that Paul takes the reader/hearer to a new locale, Antioch, in this letter.[56] The last locale was Jerusalem (2:1), where Paul was the guest and Cephas the host, but in this passage (2:11-14), Paul is the host and Cephas is the guest. Interestingly, Antioch is an important

---

53. Ibid., 231.

54. Dunn, *Epistle to the Galatians*, 116. See also Brigitte Kahl, *Galatians Re-imagined: Reading with the Eyes of the Vanquished*, Paul in Critical Contexts (Minneapolis: Fortress, 2010), 279. The location, according to Kahl, will influence the way one reads the Antioch event. The pressure toward nonconformity with the outside world will break apart the union that Paul and Cephas has established.

55. Dunn, *Epistle to the Galatians*, 116.

56. Martyn, *Galatians*, 229.

city of the Roman Empire, consisting of various identity communities,[57] and it is here, according to Paul, where the recognition of difference and its influence on hospitality come into question. As host, Paul chooses to challenge Cephas's expression of recognition and hospitality.

For instance, in the first independent clause, "I opposed him to his face," Paul confirms that he is the host and that Cephas is the guest first by pointing out that Cephas is the one visiting him in Antioch ("came to Antioch") and second by confronting him, since Paul, as host, puts his guest, Cephas, in a situation that requires delicate decisions. Cephas has entered the realm of Paul's authority,[58] and Paul puts unconditional hospitality (ethical notion) at risk. Paul takes the risk not with a casual confrontation but with a very biting confrontation (*antestēn*)—"to his face" (*kata prosōoin autō* [2:11]). Cephas will now have to risk sitting down and accepting whatever challenge is posed to him by Paul. At this point in the text, Paul does not disclose what causes this confrontation, but recognition and hospitality surely do not always imply resigning oneself to the expectations of a guest. Paul does see himself in the right[59] and thus works with an understanding of hospitality and recognition where the host and guest are no longer equal partners. Cephas's actions, which will soon be narrated, are an account of imperfect hospitality. Cephas's past actions in Antioch surely altered Paul's expectations of recognition and hospitality, upsetting him deeply regarding table fellowship or, more importantly, causing friction that created a gap between expectations and behavior among the host and the guest.[60]

Verse 12

After Paul prepares the reader/hearer of an inhospitable occurrence that led him to oppose Peter to his face, he begins to narrate what unsettled him so much. Starting with the structure of "for before certain ones came"

---

57. See Gal 1:21; cf. Acts 11:25–26; 13:1; Wayne A. Meeks, *The First Urban Christians: The Social World of the Apostle Paul* (New Haven: Yale University Press, 1983), 10–11. See also Charles B. Cousar, *Galatians*, Interpretation: A Bible Commentary for Teaching and Preaching (Atlanta: John Knox, 1982), 46.

58. Dunn, *Epistle to the* Galatians, 116.

59. Ibid.

60. Ibid., 117.

(*pro tou gar elthein tinas*), Paul places the action of the infinitive "came" (*elthein*) after the controlling verb "ate" (*synēsthien*). In other words, Cephas's eating with gentiles came before and ended when certain men from James entered the space where they were eating. Hence, Cephas and Paul once practiced an ethical notion of recognition and hospitality where all who were present were of equal worth and dignity. The temporal construction of 2:12a ("for before certain ones came") points to a time when Cephas was present in Antioch and when he was in agreement with the rules of recognition and hospitality that both understood. In the tradition of ancient hospitality, therefore, both Paul and Cephas were exchanging mutual recognition and hospitable practices.[61] We know that Paul was in Jerusalem (e.g., 2:1), where Cephas provided hospitality and recognition in the role of host, and now Paul is reciprocating such actions in the form of meal and shelter. In short, one should not dishonor the other.[62]

What happened in the past on a regular basis, as the imperfect of "ate" (*synēsthien*) suggests, is that Cephas used to eat with the gentiles (2:12b) before the folks associated with James arrived. Thus Cephas as well as those at the meal in Antioch (Paul's context) have adopted the hospitable meal practice.[63] In other words, the practice of recognition and hospitality between Paul and Cephas in the past included the sharing of a meal with both gentiles and Jews, transcending any social or religious constraints regarding eating with those of a different identity. Both Paul and Cephas resigned themselves to eating with others who emanated from different communities and customs. The passage (2:12) suggests, therefore, that Cephas was quite comfortable going against any prohibitions of eating with gentiles. Furthermore, the sharing of the meal is surely a sign that Paul has accepted Cephas as a guest, and Cephas's eating with Paul and others is a sign that Cephas accepted Paul.[64] Both suspended or moved beyond their Jewish table-fellowship traditions in Antioch and thus ate with gentile believers. However, the arrival of those associated with James was like the arrival of an uninvited guest who may bring a different set

---

61. See Carolyn Osiek and David L. Balch, *Families in the New Testament World: Households and House Churches*, The Family, Religion, and Culture (Louisville: Westminster John Knox, 1997), 39.

62. Ibid., 39.

63. Martyn, *Galatians*, 232.

64. Dunn, *Epistle to the Galatians*, 117.

of rules and conventions concerning hospitality and recognition and thus disrupt the table fellowship, as the next event suggests.

These uninvited guests are part of the circumcision party (*tous ek peritomēs*) along with Cephas (1:19; 2:9). These individuals come with a sense of authority, as if they were the hosts and Paul and the gentiles were the guests. They bring a different expectation of recognition and hospitality, thus disrupting any balance of the host–guest continuum that Paul and Cephas are playing out. As a result of these individuals' arrival at the table, Paul mentions two simultaneous actions on the part of Cephas. First, Cephas "drew back"[65] (*hypestellen*), and second, he supposedly separated (*aphōrizen*) himself from the table. Cephas decided, with the arrival of these men from James, that he would not continue following the conventions of recognition and hospitality that he previously agreed upon with Paul (2:11b). Cephas, at this moment, becomes a bad guest by not honoring the conventions of hospitality for the guest and by shaming Paul as host.

Cephas separates himself from the table-fellowship in Antioch because he "feared" (*phoboumenos*) "those from the circumcision" party (*tous ek peritomēs* [2:12c]). Paul defines this party, the men who came from James, by their Jewish (ethnic and religious) identity marker. The recognition of this identity influences how Cephas understands hospitality. Hospitality, based on the recognition of this party, is defined in a colonial fashion. No trust or partial trust exists between Paul and Cephas. This partial trust also defines the roles of hosts and guests in a rigid way by power differentials. Cephas and the men from James, who are really the guests at the table, reverse roles with Paul and the gentiles and take on the role of the host. The presence of the men from James causes Cephas to make the delicate decision of siding with the men from James and employ an exclusive notion of recognition and hospitality that extends both values only to his "own" kind (a member of the leadership and circumcision party).

This "circumcision party" is directly or indirectly forcing the host and the guest to decide which conventions of hospitality to adhere to and

---

65. See Dunn, *Epistle to the Galatians*, 119–21. Dunn argues that to say that Cephas withdrew because he was eating with gentiles is a mistake. Many gentiles and Jews did cross identity and dietary boundaries. Dunn does argue that the withdrawal from the table had to do with Cephas's acknowledgment that he was too lax in sharing food with gentiles "without asking too many questions."

which community to belong to. Fearing disruption of the host–guest continuum, Paul's interpretation of Cephas's drawing back (2:12c) suggests that Cephas is not accountable to his host, Paul, but rather to another party. The imperfect tense (descriptive imperfect) of "drew back" (*hypestellen*) and "kept himself separate" (*aphōrizen*) suggest that both actions happened simultaneously on Cephas's part.[66] Such actions show Cephas's decisiveness and little trust in Paul's understanding. The dinner guest, Cephas, draws on his understanding of recognition and hospitality rather than the host Paul's. Thus Cephas's notion does not always imply reciprocity, unless it is among those who recognize one another as equal. They do not both share the same understandings of recognition and hospitality even though both assume they are doing the work of God.

Verse 13

Cephas's withdrawal from the table also included others ("the rest of the Jews" [*hoi loipoi Ioudaioi*]).[67] As such, these other Jews also shared Cephas's conventions of recognition and hospitality. For them, recognition and hospitality continue to suggest a limited acceptance, one that excludes. Paul describes Cephas's "party" as going against some principle or law ("acted insincerely" [2:13a]);[68] thus the arrival of those affiliated with James or the rest of the "Jews" signifies an outsider's intrusion into Paul's "home," particularly concerning the "house rules" of inclusion and respect for difference. The gap between expectations and behavior is now surely wider than the time when Paul and Cephas ate together with gentiles (2:12b). This gap is reflected in Paul's reading of their actions as insincere (*hypokrisei* [2:13a]). In fact, it was so disingenuous that even Barnabas, a supporter or coworker of Paul's (2:1, 9d), followed Cephas's insincerity. Thus, Cephas, the other Jews, and Barnabas are all now part of a party whose withdrawal, caused by the arrival of "certain men from James," has created a moment of malaise and discomfort, which, ironically, is part of the confirmation

---

66. See Sam K. Williams, *Galatians*, ANTC (Nashville: Abingdon, 1997), 59.

67. Dunn argues that "Jews" there is denoting a people from Palestine/Judea (*Epistle to the Galatians*, 124).

68. Williams states: "The root meaning of Paul's verb *synhypokrinesthai* and noun *hypokrisis* is to play the part of another, like an actor on stage, and thus to pretend" (*Galatians*, 58).

that recognition and hospitality are at work. Without friction, it is difficult to see recognition and hospitality at work. In other words, the tension
between host and guest shows that both parties are working with different
understandings of recognition and hospitality at the moment. One (host)
seems to be leaning toward an "open-door" policy where all are welcomed
at the table, while the other (guest) leans toward a "closed-door" policy.
What they have in common at this moment is that both work with partial
to little trust. Partial trust is present in the sense that they are receptive
of or recognize those around the table at first, only to move from partial
trust toward little trust when certain identities and/or house rules arouse
suspicion and opposition. Recognition and hospitality are now expressed
only to their own kind or supporters. This includes Paul as well, as seen in
the final verse of this recollection.

Verse 14

In closing the recounting of the Antioch incident, Paul begins in a way
similar to how he began in 2:11. He begins with the adversative conjunction "but" (*alla*) to suggest a position in opposition to their insincerity,
followed with an adverbial conjunction, "when" (*hote*), to indicate the
time of the action ("I saw" [*eidon*]), thus amplifying that he knows for
sure now what is to follow, namely, that Cephas's party is not "straight-
forward" (*orthopodousin*) in "the truth of the gospel" (*tēn alētheian tou
euangeliou*). In other words, due to the insincerity of Cephas and other
supporters in not eating with the gentiles, Paul, playing host, understands
that Cephas's inhospitality and nonrecognition of difference is connected
to Cephas's interpretation of the truth of the gospel. The guest, Cephas,
has decided to breach etiquette and refuse Paul's hospitality and recognition of difference. Therefore, as a response to Cephas's breach, Paul
speaks to Cephas directly, "before them all" (*emprosthen pantōn*), so all
present could hear that Cephas's actions contradict his expression of recognition and hospitality. Aiming it at Cephas specifically, "you" (*sy*), Paul
finishes with a conditional question to Cephas. The question, beginning
with the particle "if" (*ei*), assumes a truth, namely, that Cephas, "though
a Jew, lives like a Gentile and not like a Jew." In other words, Paul—perhaps not entirely convinced that Cephas actually lives like a gentile, based
on Cephas's earlier insincerity at the table meal—assumes that Cephas,
a Jew who lives like a gentile, is in no position to require gentiles "to

live like Jews" (*Ioudaizein*). Cephas's actions at the table meal blatantly contradict his position. As guest, Cephas, sees his role as the guardian of Jewish norms. Yet, in a way, Paul also sees his role as host as the guardian of Jewish norms. Both assume the role of the interpreter of the gospel of recognition and hospitality as well as the guardian of the gospel of Christ. Hence, the notions of recognition and hospitality undergirding this text lead to the formation (or continual redefinition) of the meanings of these values for their respective communities. Meanings vacillate between who is the host and who is the guest, but also who is recognized or not recognized as part of the community. Paul's questioning of Cephas is thus not simply a matter of Paul offering hospitality and Cephas refusing it. I see it more as both men appealing to their understanding of recognition and hospitality to reach a shared understanding of how to share space or how to conceptualize recognition and hospitality within a new context.

Conclusion

It follows, then, that Paul and Cephas are constantly weaving in and out of different understandings of recognition and hospitality. Hospitality cannot function without recognition, since recognition opens the relationship between host and guest to respect one another first before acts of generosity are employed. By the end of 2:11–14, therefore, both Paul and Cephas fail to recognize one another and thus play out a failed hospitality scene. Both are responsible for this failure. Both, by way of aiming to be inclusive by recognizing each other and expressing hospitality toward each other, place another condition upon the other. For Paul, it is belief in the gospel of Christ (otherwise one cannot eat at the table), and for Cephas, it is belief that only those of a like cultural identity can eat together. Both Paul and Cephas see those not like themselves as the problem, rather than seeing themselves as the problem.

Such a reflection of recognition and hospitality resonates with issues of incorporating difference within established communities today. It is not identical to the cultural expression of recognition and hospitality in 2:11–14, yet it speaks to the issue of inclusion and exclusion and those conditions placed upon new arrivants within the community. For new arrivants, the question of how much of their identity to give up in order to belong to an established community is ongoing in the United States (including religious communities). This is a difficult question. As I have argued earlier, to be included must involve both the host and the guest to the point where host and guest disappear—however difficult this may be to achieve. Galatians 2:11–14 does not speak directly to modern or postmodern questions of inclusion and exclusion, yet it does not mean that such a text cannot spark thinking about our current context of inclusion and exclusion, whatever that may be. Paul and Cephas were ready to include others, yet they were not willing to give up something of their identities to allow this to happen. The Letter to the Galatians shows glimpses of recognition and hospitality, as the text of 2:11–14 demonstrated to a certain extent, yet conditions remained. To address today's question of inclusion and exclusion of migrants or ethnic/racial communities, for example, both parties must aim for mutual reciprocity of recognition and hospitality no matter who plays the host and guest. To do so allows for recognition and hospitality to be extended and practiced toward those in society who are different. If so, such an understanding may lead to all folks being both together and apart, a reimagination of what it means to be a community committed to the values of recognition and hospitality.

6

Conclusion: Latino/a Biblical Interpretation: Is It a Question of Being and/or Practice?

These chapters exploring varied strategies raise a central and intriguing issue for the critic and reader: Is identity a matter of being and/or practice? Is the Latino/a-ness of an interpretation defined by the personal identity (however named) of the interpreter? Or is it a matter of how Latino/a biblical interpretation is practiced—that is, are there certain principles, sources, methods (reading strategies), or aims that make some biblical interpretations Latino/a and others not? In this concluding discussion, it is not my intention to define Latino/a biblical interpretation in a rigid way, but rather, I aim to establish the position that Latino/a biblical interpretation is a process of becoming, understanding, and belonging, as reflected in these chapters. Such a position allows for Latino/a biblical interpretation to include more ways of being (identities) and doing (practices) and suggests a sense of inclusion rather than exclusion. Finally, the issue of intersectionality and Latino/a biblical interpretation is briefly introduced as another possible way to move forward in the field, followed by a discussion of whose recognition I am seeking in this volume.

This is a revised and updated version of an essay that appeared as "Latino/a Biblical Interpretation: A Question of Being and/or Practice?," in *Latino/a Biblical Hermeneutics: Problematics, Objectives, Strategies*, ed. Francisco Lozada Jr. and Fernando F. Segovia, SemeiaSt 68 (Atlanta: SBL Press, 2014), 365–69.

Identity

Does one have to be Latino/a to practice Latino/a biblical criticism? This is a question, as I see it, centered on whether Latino/a-ness is assumed to be an essential element of Latino/a biblical interpretation. Although this question is not directly addressed in the essays, it is surely becoming an important factor and even a guiding principle in the field. However, I would like to move the conversation away from the dichotomous logic of an either/or and toward a both/and. That is, as some of the biblical interpreters have alluded to through the foregrounding of their identities, Latino/a identity is not simply fixed but is rather both fixed and fluid. In other words, there is something fixed that identifies one as Latino/a, principally by race/ethnicity (i.e., biologically or genetically connections), by a shared language (i.e., Spanish), or by a geographical cultural heritage (i.e., cultural home in Latin America). Yet there is also something fluid that identifies one as Latino/a by way of, for example, a shared commitment, experience, or acquired language. The fixity of Latino/a identity varies, but it is often linked to some notion of innateness (full or mixed ethnic/racial identities, birthplace of origins, or language) or experience. The fluidity of Latino/a identity may also vary, but it is linked to some notion of purpose (commitment to the Latino/a community, being in a committed relationship with a Latino/a, or agreeing with Latino/a political causes). The interplay of the factors of fixity and fluidity comprising the Latino/a identity is a negotiation. At times, it is not even a negotiation. A fixed identity or a fluid identity is thrown upon you whether you like it or not. My point here is that both ends of the spectrum (fixity/fluidity) challenge each other and, at the same time, are part of the processual development of Latino/a identity.

This question of what constitutes Latino/a identity is increasingly important given the rise of migration from Latin America to the United States. It will become even more significant as second- and third-generation Latinos/as identify themselves as Latinos/as and the number of Latinos/as of mixed ethnic/racial backgrounds and differentiated gender and sexuality identities grow. The question of identity is particularly important here because it suggests another, deeper question—namely, what brings these chapters together under the construct *Latino/a*? Is it a sense of commonality or shared identity? Is it a set of shared beliefs and commitments? Is it because I identify myself as Latino? Or is it because I share some common political purpose, as some other communities have done in the past (e.g., feminists)? Said another way, is there an underlying sense of oneness that links my readings with other Latino/a biblical interpretations?

What seems to be certain is that many Latino/a biblical interpretations have at their core a sense of mutuality or commonality for the sake of the good of the Latino/a community. This type of common identity, both fixed and fluid, engenders a sense of community (a safe place to explore) that supports various Latino/a identities but also leaves space for disagreements. Far from being dangerous or destructive, this enables Latinos/as to further develop and advance their own specific ideas and conceptualizations and ultimately shape the entire field of Latino/a biblical scholarship and in biblical interpretation. Is this shared sense of commitment toward the Latino/a community another possible guiding principle of the field? In my assessment, Latino/a biblical interpretation seems to indicate that it may be.

The question of identity, therefore, surely encompasses more than falling within fixed lines of identification. The question must extend to issues of purpose and commitment as well. This makes defining Latino/a biblical interpretation a much more complex and nuanced task. Partially, this is also why I prefer not to endorse a fixed definition. In fact, the danger of endorsing a fixed definition is that it may involve excluding identities that seem to contradict the desired totality of a unified (community) identity—particularly if those identities do not reflect the normative views of what constitutes a Latino/a. In other words, to not define is to invite, rather than displace, the outsider. To not define avoids constructing an impermeable border that can often cause fields to become static and exclusive, rather than fluid and open. It challenges a notion of identity that may be used to define legitimate work by deciding who belongs and who does not, who speaks the same language and who does not, and who holds the same assumptions and principles and who does not. That said, the danger of not defining, even broadly, is that others outside the community or non-Latinos/as will do the defining. The chapters in this volume exemplify the process of defining a Latino/a identity in a state of becoming—an engagement that requires and thus is open to constant negotiation with the goal of understanding and belonging.

Practice

In addition to the question of identity (fixed and/or fluid), some Latino/a biblical interpretations have focused on the question of practice (or reading strategy) as a strong element that determines what constitutes Latino/a biblical interpretation. In other words, they suggest that what makes Latino/a biblical interpretation *Latino/a* is how it is done. As most of the essays note, one aspect of this reading strategy is the foregrounding of Latino/a identity and its reality. This foregrounding of Latino/a identity challenges normative (Eurocentric) ways of doing biblical interpretation. The foregrounding or positioning of Latino/a identity carries with it the possibility of discovering new meanings of a text, discovering new ways of thinking about a text, or introducing new knowledge and identities to the text. In addition, the foregrounding of Latino/a identity as a reading strategy does not necessarily restrict the practice of Latino/a biblical interpretation to Latinos/as only. Indeed, it implies that by using this reading strategy, Latino/a interpretations can be conducted by anyone who feels connected or committed to the Latino/a community. However, there is cause for concern in the assumption that Latino/a identity is not defined by identity but rather by practice, in that it opens the door for anyone to do Latino/a biblical interpretation. One unfortunate outcome of this assumption could be that concerns, issues, or questions that are particular to the Latino/a community are overlooked or ignored. In addition, it may also lead to the assumption that anyone can be inextricably bound to the Latino/a community by the very fact of producing a Latino/a reading and thus appear to be a part of the Latino/a community, but it does not acknowledge that they always have an "out"—not being Latino/a by way of ethnic/racial identification.

Some sense of what Latino/a biblical interpretation is (or is not) is always at work in the decisions being made during the reading experience. Likewise, publishers, schools, and courses make judgments regarding the nature of Latino/a biblical scholarship. Even in the field, some scholars suggest that Latino/a biblical interpretation is better defined by the practice of it, thus promoting the inclusion of all those empathetic with the Latino/a community or connected directly with the Latino/a community to the practice of Latino/a biblical interpretation. I suggest that perhaps neither being nor practice by itself is the best way to define what Latino/a biblical interpretation is. Instead, a combination of both—something fixed and something fluid—may provide the best fit. In this sense, one could argue that the practice of Latino/a biblical interpretation is not simply about the foregrounding of Latino/a identity; it is also about challenging the idea that there is a proper way of doing Latino/a biblical interpretation. The chapters in this volume support this notion—that there is no single correct way of practicing Latino/a biblical interpretation. Rather, they note that Latino/a biblical interpretation has taken multifarious forms; has focused on different issues and texts; and has drawn from a variety of theoretical positions, sources, methods, and reading strategies. Latino/a biblical readings can and do change over time as readers, cultures, and politics change. It is a practice that represents the ever-changing relations between readers, texts, and the world. As such, the answer to what Latino/a biblical interpretation is remains open for discussion. What is eminently clear, however, is that Latino/a biblical interpretation is a field that continues to evolve and *become*.

Looking Forward

In moving forward with Latino/a biblical interpretation, perhaps it would be helpful to shift the focus of inquiry from determining what it is to how it constructs knowledge, which in turn constructs identities and practices. One way to challenge both of these elements—being and practice—is to focus on the intersectionality of race/ethnicity, sexual, gender, and class identities. A focus on this area presents challenges to any notion of a homogenized identity on which Latino/a biblical interpretation might be perceived to be founded and calls instead for a reading strategy based on intersectional analyses of Latino/a identity and its relation to systems of power/knowledge. Intersectionality also challenges any singular way of doing Latino/a biblical interpretation as canon. The complex interaction between, for example, race and sexuality calls for a variety of ways of doing Latino/a biblical interpretation. Conversely, insisting that there is only one way of doing Latino/a biblical interpretation limits not only the reading strategies but also the way we think about Latinos/as.

This is not to say that intersectionality is the only strategy one may use to explore or do Latino/a biblical interpretation.[2] Intersectionality also has

---

2. See Robyn Henderson-Espinoza, "Queer Theory and Latina/o Theologiz-

its limitations. For instance, it may lead to a lowered level of vigilance and commitment to looking at crucial questions of the ethnic/racial formation of Latinos/as—for example, through the lens of another optic such as class, sexual orientation, or religion—and thus possibly make Latinos/as an abstraction or a blurring of difference. In other words, race/ethnicity does not circumscribe these other identities, nor do these other identities circumscribe race/ethnicity. They are all intertwined. The same goes for the reading practices. The issue of intersectionality is one among many other foci that Latino/a biblical interpretation will need to engage head-on in the near future in order to move away from an assimilationist understanding of sameness (one way of being and doing Latino/a biblical interpretation) toward a liberationist understanding of choice (multiple ways of being and doing Latino/a biblical interpretation).

What is more, another question emerges in Latino/a biblical interpretation (as well as other minoritized interpretations): whose recognition are we (Latinos/as) seeking in doing biblical interpretation: the academy or the community? I am of the position that it is both. Some Latino/a biblical interpretation is done to seek recognition from the academy. Otherwise, by not including your interpretation in the history of interpretation, that cultural interpretation may be written out. Also, seeking recognition from the academy allows Latino/a biblical interpretation to push the boundaries of how biblical interpretation is conceived and practiced, as discussed in the introduction. It challenges any assumptions that may suppress the agency of the Latinos/as in doing interpretation. At the same time, Latino/a biblical interpretation is written for the transformation of the community. This notion of transformation may vary. I am particularly interested in the questions of representation, identification, and belongingness. These aspects are similar to what one finds in Latino/a studies overall. What is important to state here is that Latino/a biblical interpretation, for me, does not have to seek recognition from both the academy and the community at the same time. There are some Latino/a interpreters who focus on either one or the other audience for whatever reasons, and that is fine.

---

ing," in Espín, *Wiley Blackwell Companion to Latino/a Theology*, 329–46. For an excellent example in biblical studies, see Tat-siong Benny Liew, "Queering Closets and Perverting Desires: Cross-Examining John's Engendering and Transgendering Word across Different Worlds," in Bailey, Liew, and Segovia, *They Were All Together*, 251–88.

There is some question whether Latino/a interpretation should abandon the academy altogether because by participating in the it as a minoritized group, Latino/a interpretation only reifies the oppressive practices of the academy. Even though this position has some merit, it does not challenge the center. One ends up being a foreigner with legal status and never really belonging in the history. Nonetheless, the position of leaving the academy altogether begs for further exploration.

Bibliography

Agosto, Efraín. "The Letter to the Philippians." Pages 281–93 in *A Postcolonial Commentary on the New Testament Writings*. Edited by Fernando F. Segovia and R. S. Sugirtharajah. Bible and Postcolonialism 13. London: T&T Clark, 2007.

———. "Paul vs. Empire: A Postcolonial and Latino Reading." *Perspectivas: Occasional Papers* 6 (2002): 37–56.

———. "Reading the Word in America: US Latino/a Religious Communities and Their Scriptures." Pages 117–64 in *MisReading America: Scriptures and Difference*. Edited by Vincent L. Wimbush with the assistance of Lalruatkima and Melissa Renee Reid. Oxford: Oxford University Press, 2010.

———. "Sola Scriptura and Latino/a Protestant Hermeneutics: An Exploration." Pages in 69–87 in *Building Bridges, Doing Justice: Constructing a Latino/a Ecumenical Theology*. Edited by Orlando O. Espín. Maryknoll, NY: Orbis Books, 2009.

Aichele, George. "The Translator's Dilemma: A Response to Boer, Coker, Elliott, and Nadella." Pages 59–65 in *Ideology, Culture, and Translation*. Edited by Scott S. Elliott and Roland Boer. SemeiaSt 69. Atlanta: Society of Biblical Literature, 2012.

Álvarez, Julia. *How the García Girls Lost Their Accent*. New York: Plume, 1992.

Appleby, Joyce, Lynn Hunt, and Margaret Jacob. *Telling the Truth about History*. New York: Norton, 1994.

Aquino, María Pilar. *Our Cry for Life: Feminist Theology from Latin America*. Translated by Dinah Livingstone. Maryknoll, NY: Orbis Books, 1993.

Arterbury, Andrew. *Entertaining Angels: Early Christian Hospitality in its Mediterranean Setting*. NTM 8. Sheffield: Sheffield Phoenix, 2005.

Avalos, Hector. "Rethinking Latino Hermeneutics: An Atheist Perspective." Pages 59–72 in *Latino/a Biblical Hermeneutics: Problematics, Objectives, Strategies*. SemeiaSt 68. Edited by Francisco Lozada Jr. and Fernando F. Segovia. Atlanta: SBL Press, 2014.

———. *Strangers in Our Own Land: Religion in U.S. Latina/o Literature*. Nashville: Abingdon, 2005.

Bacon, Benjamin W. *Studies in Matthew*. London: Constable, 1930.

Bailey, Randall C., Tat-Siong Benny Liew, and Fernando F. Segovia, eds. *They Were All Together in One Place? Toward Minority Biblical Criticism*. SemeiaSt 57. Atlanta: Society of Biblical Literature, 2009.

Balabanski, Vicky. "An Earth Bible Reading of the Lord's Prayer: Matthew 6.9–13." Pages 151–61 in *Readings from the Perspective of the Earth*. Earth Bible 1. Edited by Norman C. Habel. Sheffield: Sheffield Academic, 2000.

Barr, James. *The Semantics of Biblical Language*. Oxford: Oxford University Press, 1961.

Blackshaw, Tony. *Key Concepts in Community Studies*. SAGE Key Concepts. London: Sage, 2010.

Boff, Leonardo. *Jesus Christ Liberator: A Critical Christology for Our Time*. Maryknoll, NY: Orbis Books, 1978.

Boring, M. Eugene. "The Gospel of Matthew: Introduction, Commentary and Reflection." *NIB* 8:89–505.

Botta, Alejandro F. "What Does It Mean to Be a Latino Biblical Critic? A Brief Essay." Pages 107–19 in *Latino/a Biblical Hermeneutics: Problematics, Objectives, Strategies*. Edited by Francisco Lozada Jr. and Fernando F. Segovia. SemeiaSt 68. Atlanta: SBL Press, 2014.

Brettell, Caroline B., and Faith G. Nibbs. "Immigrant Suburban Settlement and the 'Threat' to Middle Class Status and Identity: The Case of Farmers Branch, Texas." *International Migration* 49 (2011): 1–30.

Brooks, James A., and Carlton L. Winbery. *Syntax of New Testament Greek*. Lanham, MD: University Press of America, 1979.

Burrus, Virginia. "Augustine's Bible." Pages 69–82 in *Ideology, Culture, and Translation*. Edited by Scott S. Elliott and Roland Boer. SemeiaSt 69. Atlanta: Society of Biblical Literature, 2012.

Busto, Rudy V. "'It Really Resembled an Earthly Paradise': Reading Motolinía's Account of the Caída de nuestros primeros padres." *BibInt* 2 (1994): 111–37.

Cantú, Lionel, Jr. *The Sexuality of Migration: Border Crossings and Mexican Immigrant Men*. Edited by Nancy A. Naples and Salvador Vidal Ortiz.

Intersections: Transdisciplinary Perspectives on Genders and Sexualities. New York: New York University Press, 2009.

Carroll R., M. Daniel. *Christians at the Border: Immigration, the Church, and the Bible*. Grand Rapids: Baker Academic, 2008.

Carter, Warren. *John and Empire: Initial Explorations*. New York: T&T Clark, 2008.

———. *Matthew and Empire: Initial Explorations*. Harrisburg, PA: Trinity Press International, 2001.

Castles, Stephen, and Mark J. Miller. *The Age of Migration: International Population Movements in the Modern World*. 4th ed. New York: Guilford, 2009.

Copher, Julia Ortiz. *The Line of the Sun*. Athens: University of Georgia Press, 1991.

Cortés-Fuentes, David. "Not Like the Gentiles: The Characterization of Gentiles in the Gospel according to St. Matthew." *JHLT* 9 (2001): 6–26.

Cousar, Charles B. *Galatians*. Interpretation: A Bible Commentary for Teaching and Preaching. Atlanta: John Knox, 1982.

Culpepper, R. Alan. *Anatomy of the Fourth Gospel: A Study of Literary Design*. Philadelphia: Fortress, 1983.

Daston, Lorraine, and Peter Galison, *Objectivity*. New York: Zone, 2010.

Derrida, Jacques. *Of Hospitality*. Translated by Rachel Bowlby. Stanford, CA: Stanford University Press, 2000.

Dube, Musa W. *Postcolonial Feminist Interpretation of the Bible*. St. Louis, MO: Chalice, 2000.

Duling, Dennis C., and Norman Perrin. *The New Testament: Proclamation and Parenesis, Myth and History*. 3rd ed. New York: Harcourt, Brace, 1994.

Dunn, James D. G. *The Epistle to the Galatians*. Black's New Testament Commentary. Peabody, MA: Hendrickson, 1993.

Elizondo, Virgilio. *Galilean Journey: The Mexican-American Promise*. Maryknoll, NY: Orbis Books, 1983.

Esler, Philip. *Galatians*. New Testament Readings. London: Routledge, 1998.

Felder, Cain Hope, ed. *Stony the Road We Trod: African American Biblical Interpretation*. Minneapolis: Fortress, 1991.

Fernandez, Eleazar S., and Fernando F. Segovia, eds. *A Dream Unfinished: Theological Reflections on America from the Margins*. Eugene, OR: Wipf & Stock, 2006.

Findlay, Eileen J. Suárez. *We Are Left without a Father Here: Masculinity, Domesticity, and Migration in Postwar Puerto Rico*. American Encounters/Global Interactions. Durham, NC: Duke University Press, 2014.

Fraser, Nancy, and Axel Honneth. "Introduction: Redistribution or Recognition?" Pages 1–5 in *Redistribution or Recognition? A Political-Philosophical Exchange*. Edited by Nancy Fraser and Axel Honneth. Translated by Joel Golb, James Ingram, and Christiane Wilke. London: Verso, 2003.

Gadamer, Hans-Georg. "The Universality of the Hermeneutical Problem." Edited and translated by David Linge. Pages 179–89 in *The Interpretation of Texts*. Vol. 1 of *Hermeneutical Inquiry*. Edited by David E. Klemm. AARSR 43. Atlanta: Scholars Press, 1986.

Garcia, Cristina. *Dreaming in Cuban*. New York: Ballantine, 1993.

García-Alfonso, Cristina. "El silencio del cuerpo: La historia de Tamar." Pages 31–42 in *Camino a Emaús: Compartiendo el ministerio de Jesús*. Edited by Ada María Isasi-Díaz, Timoteo Matovina, and Nina M. Torres-Vidal. Minneapolis: Fortress, 2002.

García-Treto, Francisco. "Exile in the Hebrew Bible: A Postcolonial Look from the Cuban Diaspora." Pages 65–78 in *They Were All Together in One Place? Toward Minority Biblical Criticism*. Edited by Randall C. Bailey, Tat-Siong Benny Liew, and Fernando F. Segovia. SemeiaSt 57. Atlanta: Society of Biblical Literature, 2009.

George, Roji T. *Paul's Identity in Galatians: A Postcolonial Appraisal*. New Delhi, India: Christian World Imprints, 2016.

Gibson, Jeffrey B. *The Disciples' Prayer: The Prayer Jesus Taught in Its Historical Setting*. Minneapolis: Fortress, 2015.

Gonzalez, Juan. *Harvest of Empire: A History of Latinos in America*. Rev. ed. New York: Penguin, 2011.

González, Justo L. *Mañana: Christian Theology from a Hispanic Perspective*. Nashville: Abingdon, 1990.

———. *Santa Biblia: The Bible through Hispanic Eyes*. Nashville: Abingdon, 1996.

Grant, Robert M., with David Tracy. *A Short History of the Interpretation of the Bible*. 2nd ed., rev. and enl. Philadelphia: Fortress, 1984.

Guardiola-Sáenz, Leticia A. "Border-Crossing and Its Redemptive Power in John 7:53–8:11: A Cultural Reading of Jesus and the *Accused*." Pages 129–52 in *John and Postcolonialism: Travel, Space and Power*. Edited by Musa W. Dube and Jeffrey L. Staley. Bible and Postcolonialism 7. Sheffield: Sheffield Academic, 2002.

———. "Jesus the Borderlander: Hybridity as Survival Strategy and Model for Political Change: A Cultural Representation from the Gospel of John." PhD diss., Vanderbilt University, 2009.

Gutiérrez, David G., ed. *The Columbia History of Latinos in the United States since 1960.* New York: Columbia University Press, 2004.

Habermas, Jürgen. "Towards a Theory of Communicative Competence." Pages 209–34 in *The Interpretation of Existence.* Vol. 2 of *Hermeneutical Inquiry.* Edited by David E. Klemm. AARSR 44. Repr., Atlanta: Scholars Press, 1986.

Haswell, Richard, and Janis Haswell. *Hospitality as Authoring: An Essay for the English Profession.* Boulder, CO: Utah State University Press, 2015.

Henderson-Espinoza, Robyn. "Queer Theory and Latina/o Theologizing." Pages 329–46 in *The Wiley Blackwell Companion to Latino/a Theology.* Edited by Orlando O. Espín. Malden, MA: Wiley-Blackwell, 2015.

Hidalgo, Jacqueline M. "Reading from No Place: Toward a Hybrid and Ambivalent Study." Pages 165–86 in *Latino/a Biblical Hermeneutics: Problematics, Objectives, Strategies.* Edited by Francisco Lozada Jr. and Fernando F. Segovia. SemeiaSt 68. Atlanta: SBL Press, 2014.

———. *Revelation in Aztlán: Scriptures, Utopias, and the Chicano Movement.* The Bible and Cultural Studies. New York: Palgrave Macmillan, 2016.

Houston, Fleur S. *You Shall Love the Stranger as Yourself: The Bible, Refugees, and Asylum.* New York: Routledge, 2015.

Isasi-Díaz, Ada María. *Mujerista Theology: A Theology for the Twenty-First Century.* Maryknoll, NY: Orbis Books, 1996.

Jiménez, Francisco. *The Circuit: Stories from the Life of a Migrant Child.* Albuquerque: University of New Mexico Press, 1997.

Jiménez, Pablo. "The Bible: A Hispanic Perspective." Pages 66–79 in *Teología en conjunto: A Collaborative Hispanic Protestant Theology.* Edited by José David Rodriguez and Loida I. Martell-Otero. Louisville: Westminster John Knox, 1997.

———. "In Search of a Hispanic Model of Biblical Interpretation." *JHLT* 3 (1995): 66–79.

Kahl, Brigitte. *Galatians Re-imagined: Reading with the Eyes of the Vanquished.* Paul in Critical Contexts. Minneapolis: Fortress, 2010.

Kennedy, George A. *New Testament Interpretation through Rhetorical Criticism.* SR. Chapel Hill: University of North Carolina Press, 1984.

Kevern, Peter. "Translation Theory." Pages 56–62 in *Searching for Meaning:*

An Introduction to Interpreting the New Testament. Edited by Paula Gooder. Louisville: Westminster John Knox, 2009.

Kingbury, Jack Dean. *Matthew as Story.* Philadelphia: Fortress, 1988.

———. *Matthew: Structure, Christology, Kingdom.* Philadelphia: Fortress, 1975.

Klemm, David E. Introduction to *The Interpretation of Texts.* Vol. 1 of *Hermeneutical Inquiry.* Edited by David E. Klemm. AARSR 43. Atlanta: Scholars Press, 1986.

Koenig, John. *New Testament Hospitality: Partnerships with Strangers as Promise and Mission.* OBT 17. Philadelphia: Fortress, 1985.

Latin-English Booklet Missal for Praying the Traditional Mass. 4th ed. Glenview, IL: Coalition in Support of *Ecclesia Dei,* 2009.

Liew, Tat-Siong Benny. "Queering Closets and Perverting Desires: Cross-Examining John's Engendering and Transgendering Word across Different Worlds." Pages 251–88 in *They Were All Together in One Place? Toward Minority Biblical Criticism.* Edited by Randall C. Bailey, Tat-Siong Benny Liew, and Fernando F. Segovia. SemeiaSt 57. Atlanta: Society of Biblical Literature, 2009.

———. *What Is Asian American Biblical Hermeneutics? Reading the New Testament.* Intersections: Asian and Pacific American Transcultural Studies. Honolulu: University of Hawaii Press, 2007.

Lipsitz, George. *How Racism Takes Place.* Philadelphia: Temple University Press, 2011.

Lozada, Francisco, Jr. "The Bible as a Text in Cultures: Latinas/os." Pages 37–43 in *The Peoples' Bible: New Revised Standard Version with the Apocrypha.* Edited by Curtiss Paul DeYoung, Wilda C. Gafney, Leticia A Guardiola-Sáenz, George Tinker, and Frank M. Yamada. Minneapolis: Fortress Press, 2009.

———. "Journey and the Fourth Gospel: A Latino/a Exploration." *Int* 65 (2011): 264–75.

———. "Latino/a Biblical Interpretation: A Question of Being and/or Practice?" Pages 365–69 in *Latino/a Biblical Hermeneutics: Problematics, Objectives, Strategies.* Edited by Francisco Lozada Jr. and Fernando F. Segovia. SemeiaSt 68. Atlanta: SBL Press, 2014.

———. *A Literary Reading of John 5: Text as Construction.* New York: Lang, 2000.

———. "Matthew 6:9b–13 (The Lord's Prayer): Explorations into a Latino/a Optic on Language and Translation." Pages 271–85 in *Matthew.* Edited by Nicole Wilkinson Duran and James Grimshaw. Texts @ Contexts. Minneapolis: Fortress, 2013.

———. "Narrative Identities of the Gospel of John." Pages 341–50 in *The Oxford Handbook to Biblical Narrative*. Edited by Danna Nolan Fewell. Oxford: Oxford University Press, 2015.

———. "Toward Latino/a Biblical Studies: Foregrounding Identities and Transforming Communities." Pages 187–202 in *Latino/a Biblical Hermeneutics: Problematics, Objectives, Strategies*. Edited by Francisco Lozada Jr. and Fernando F. Segovia. SemeiaSt 68. Atlanta: SBL Press, 2014.

Lozada, Francisco, Jr., and Fernando F. Segovia, eds. *Latino/a Biblical Hermeneutics: Problematics, Objectives, Strategies*, SemeiaSt 68. Atlanta: SBL Press, 2014.

Luibhéld, Eithne. "Introduction: Queering Migration and Citizenship." Pages ix–xlvi in *Queer Migrations: Sexuality, U.S. Citizenship, and Border Crossings*. Edited by Eithne Luibhéid and Lionel Cantú Jr. Minneapolis: University of Minnesota Press, 2005.

Luibhéid, Eithne, and Lionel Cantú Jr., eds. *Queer Migrations: Sexuality, U.S. Citizenship, and Border Crossings*. Minneapolis: University of Minnesota Press, 2005.

Machado, Daisy L. "The Unnamed Woman: Justice, Feminists, and the Undocumented Woman." Pages in 161–76 in *A Reader in Latina Feminist Theology: Religion and Justice*. Edited by María Pilar Aquino, Daisy L. Machado, and Jeanette Rodríguez. Austin: University of Texas Press, 2002.

Maldonado, Robert D. "¿La Conquista? Latin American (*Mestizaje*) Reflections on the Biblical Conquest." *JHLT* 2 (1995): 5–25.

———. "Reading Malinche Reading Ruth: Toward a Hermeneutics of Betrayal." *Semeia* 72 (1995): 91–110.

Martyn, J. Louis. *Galatians: A New Translation with Introduction and Commentary*. AB 33A. New York: Doubleday, 1997.

Medina, Néstor. *Mestizaje: (Re)Mapping Race, Culture, and Faith in Latina/o Catholicism*. Studies in Latino/a Catholicism. Maryknoll, NY: Orbis Books, 2009.

Meeks, Wayne A. *The First Urban Christians: The Social World of the Apostle Paul*. New Haven: Yale University Press, 1983.

———. *The Origins of Christian Morality*. New Haven: Yale University Press, 1993.

Mena-López, Maricel. "Because of an Ethiopian Woman: Reflections on Race, Gender, and Religion in the Biblical World." Pages 145–65 in *Feminist Intercultural Theology: Latina Explorations for a Just World.* Edited by María Pilar Aquino and Maria José Rosado-Nunes. Studies in Latino/a Catholicism. Maryknoll, NY: Orbis Books, 2007.

Molina, Natalia. *How Race Is Made in America: Immigration, Citizenship, and the Historical Power of Racial Scripts.* American Crossroads 38. Berkeley: University of California Press, 2014.

Nava, Gregory, dir. *El Norte.* New York: Public Broadcasting Service, 1984.

Oden, Amy C. ed. *And You Welcomed Me: A Sourcebook on Hospitality in Early Christianity.* Nashville: Abingdon, 2001.

Ogletree, Thomas W. *Hospitality to the Stranger: Dimensions of Moral Understanding.* Philadelphia: Fortress, 1985.

Osiek, Carolyn, and David L. Balch. *Families in the New Testament World: Households and House Churches.* The Family, Religion, and Culture. Louisville: Westminster John Knox, 1997.

Palmer, Richard E. *Hermeneutics: Interpretation Theory in Schleiermacher, Dilthey, Heidegger, and Gadamer.* Northwestern University Studies in Phenomenology and Existential Philosophy. Evanston, IL: Northwestern University Press, 1969.

Perissinotto, Giorgio. "Linguistic Constraints, Programmatic Fit, and Political Correctness: The Case of Spanish in the United States." Pages 171–87 in *Critical Latin American and Latino Studies.* Edited by Juan Poblete. Cultural Studies of the Americas 12. Minneapolis: University of Minnesota Press, 2003.

Pohl, Christine D. *Making Room: Recovering Hospitality as a Christian Tradition.* Grand Rapids: Eerdmans, 1999.

Punt, Jeremy. "'The Others' in Galatians." Pages 45–54 in *Soundings in Cultural Criticism: Perspectives and Methods in Culture, Power, and Identity in the New Testament.* Edited by Francisco Lozada Jr. and Greg Carey. Soundings. Minneapolis: Fortress, 2013.

Recinos, Harold J. *Good News from the Barrio: Prophetic Witness for the Church.* Louisville: Westminster John Knox, 2006.

Reimer, Ivoni Richter. "The Forgiveness of Debts in Matthew and Luke: For an Economy without Exclusions." Pages 152–68 in *God's Economy: Biblical Studies from Latin America.* Edited by Ross Kinsler and Gloria Kinsler. Maryknoll, NY: Orbis Books, 2005.

Reinhartz, Adele. *Befriending the Beloved Disciple: A Jewish Reading of the Gospel of John.* New York: Continuum, 2001.

Reventlow, Henning Graf. *History of Biblical Interpretation.* Translated by Leo G. Purdue and Jim Duke. 4 vols. RBS 50, 61–63. Atlanta: Society of Biblical Literature, 2009–2010.

Ricoeur, Paul. "Existence and Hermeneutics." Edited by Don Ihde. Translated by Kathleen McLaughlin. Pages 185–202 in *The Interpretation of Existence.* Vol. 2 of *Hermeneutical Inquiry.* Edited by David E. Klemm. AARSR 44. Atlanta: Scholars Press, 1986.

Rodríguez, Clara. *Changing Race: Latinos, the Census, and the History of Ethnicity in the United States.* Critical America. New York: New York University Press, 2000.

Rodriguez, Richard. *Hunger of Memory: The Education of Richard Rodriguez; An Autobiography.* New York: Bantam, 1982.

Rohena-Madrazo, Marcos. "Superlative Movement in Puerto Rican Spanish and General Spanish." *NYU Working Papers in Linguistics* 1 (2007): 1–31.

Romero, Gilbert C. *Hispanic Devotional Piety: Tracing Biblical Roots.* Maryknoll, NY: Orbis Books, 1991.

Rosello, Mireille. *Postcolonial Hospitality: The Immigrant as Guest.* Stanford, CA: Stanford University Press, 2001.

Ruiz, Jean-Pierre. "The Bible and Latino/a Theology." Pages 111–27 in *The Wiley Blackwell Companion to Latino/a Theology.* Edited by Orlando O. Espín. Malden, MA: Wiley-Blackwell, 2015.

———. *Readings from the Edges: The Bible and People on the Move.* Studies in Latino/a Catholicism. Maryknoll, NY: Orbis Books, 2011.

Russell, Letty M. *Just Hospitality: God's Welcome in a World of Difference.* Edited by J. Shannon Clarkson and Kate M. Ott. Louisville: Westminster John Knox, 2009.

Sánchez, David. *From Patmos to the Barrio: Subverting Imperial Myths.* Minneapolis: Fortress, 2008.

Schüssler Fiorenza, Elisabeth. *Jesus and the Politics of Interpretation.* New York: Continuum, 2000.

Schüssler Fiorenza, Elisabeth, and Kent H. Richards, eds. *Transforming Graduate Biblical Education: Ethos and Discipline.* GPBS 10. Atlanta: Society of Biblical Literature, 2010.

Segovia, Fernando F. "Hispanic American Theology and the Bible: Effective Weapon and Faithful Ally." Pages 21–49 in *We Are a People! Initiatives in Hispanic American Theology.* Edited by Roberto S. Goizueta. Minneapolis: Fortress, 1992.

————. "Inclusion and Exclusion in John 17: An Intercultural Reading." Pages 183–210 in *Literary and Social Readings of the Fourth Gospel*. Vol. 2 of *"What Is John?"* Edited by Fernando F. Segovia. SymS 3. Atlanta: Scholars Press, 1998.

————. "John 1:1–18 as Entrée into Johannine Reality." Pages 33–64 in *Word, Theology, and Community in John*. Edited by John Painter, R. Alan Culpepper, and Fernando F. Segovia. St. Louis, MO: Chalice, 2002.

————. "The Journey(s) of the Word of God: A Reading of the Plot of the Fourth Gospel." *Semeia* 53 (1991): 23–54.

————. "Poetics of Minority Biblical Criticism: Identification and Theorization." Pages 279–311 in *Prejudice and Christian Beginnings: Investigating Race, Gender, and Ethnicity in Early Christian Studies*. Edited by Laura Nasrallah and Elisabeth Schüssler Fiorenza. Minneapolis: Fortress, 2009.

————. "Reading Across: Intercultural Criticism and Textual Posture." Pages 59–83 in *Interpreting beyond Borders*. Edited by Fernando F. Segovia. Bible and Postcolonialism 3. Sheffield: Sheffield Academic, 2000.

————. "Toward Latino/a American Biblical Criticism: Latin(o/a)ness as Problematic." Pages 193–223 in *They Were All Together in One Place? Toward Minority Biblical Criticism*. Edited by Randall C. Bailey, Tat-Siong Benny Liew, and Fernando F. Segovia. SemeiaSt 57. Atlanta: Society of Biblical Literature, 2009.

Simonet, Miquel, Marcos Rohena-Madrazo, and Mercedes Paz. "Preliminary Evidence for Incomplete Neutralization of Coda Liquids in Puerto Rican Spanish." Pages 72–86 in *Selected Proceedings of the Third Conference on Laboratory Approaches to Spanish Phonology*. Edited by Laura Colantoni and Jeffrey Steele. Somerville, MA: Cascadilla Proceedings Project, 2008.

Sobrino, Jon. *Jesus the Liberator: A Historical-Theological Reading of Jesus of Nazareth*. Maryknoll, NY: Orbis Books, 1994.

Staley, Jeffrey L., and Musa W. Dube, eds. *John and Postcolonialism: Travel, Space and Power*. Bible and Postcolonialism 7. Sheffield: Sheffield Academic, 2002.

Stavans, Illan. *Spanglish: The Making of a New American Language*. New York: HarperCollins, 2003.

Sugirtharajah, R. S. "Blotting the Master's Copy: Locating Bible Translations." Pages 155–78 in *Postcolonial Criticism and Biblical Interpretation.*
Oxford: Oxford University Press, 2002.

———. "Textual Cleansings: A Move from the Colonial to the Postcolonial
Version." *Semeia* 76 (1996): 7–19.

Tamez, Elsa. *Against Machismo.* Yorktown Heights, NY: Meyer-Stone,
1987.

———. *The Amnesty of Grace: Justification by Faith from a Latin American Perspective.* Translated by Sharon H. Ringe. Nashville: Abingdon,
1993.

Tan, Yak-Hwee. "The Johannine Community: Caught in 'Two Worlds.'"
Pages 167–79 in *New Currents through John: A Global Perspective.*
Edited by Francisco Lozada Jr. and Tom Thatcher. RBS 54. Atlanta:
Society of Biblical Literature, 2006.

Thiselton, Anthony C. *Hermeneutics: An Introduction.* Grand Rapids:
Eerdmans, 2009.

Tolbert, Mary Ann. "Writing History, Writing Culture, Writing Ourselves."
Pages 17–30 in *Soundings in Cultural Criticism: Perspectives and Methods in Culture, Power, and Identity in the New Testament.* Edited by
Francisco Lozada Jr. and Greg Carey. Soundings. Minneapolis: Fortress, 2013.

Vena, Osvaldo D. "El Sur También Existe: A Proposal for Dialogue
between Latin American and Latino/a Hermeneutics." Pages 297–319
in *Latino/a Biblical Hermeneutics: Problematics, Objectives, Strategies.*
Edited by Francisco Lozada Jr. and Fernando F. Segovia. SemeiaSt 68.
Atlanta: SBL Press, 2014.

———. "My Hermeneutical Journey and Daily Journey into Hermeneutics:
Meaning-Making and Biblical Interpretation in the North American
Diaspora." Pages 84–106 in *Interpreting beyond Borders.* Edited by
Fernando F. Segovia. Bible and Postcolonialism 3. Sheffield: Sheffield
Academic, 2000.

Wallace, Daniel B. *Greek Grammar: Beyond the Basics.* Grand Rapids:
Zondervan, 1996.

Williams, Sam K. *Galatians.* ANTC. Nashville: Abingdon, 1997.

Young, Frances M. *Biblical Exegesis and the Formation of the Christian Culture.* Grand Rapids: Baker Academic, 1997.

Young, Robert J. C. *Postcolonialism: A Very Short Introduction.* Oxford:
Oxford University Press, 2003.

Young, Robert M., dir. *Alambrista.* Beverly Hills, CA: Filmhaus, 1979.

Zambrana, Ruth Enid. *Latinos in American Society: Families and Communities in Transition*. Ithaca, NY: Cornell University Press, 2011.

Ancient Sources Index

Author Index

Subject Index

assimilation, 3, 13, 25, 48, 62, 65–66, 76, 116
American Dream, 66 n. 8, 73
being and/or practice, 17, 111
belongingness, 14–15, 21–22, 42, 49–50, 52–53, 53 n. 19, 55, 59, 116
biblical as concept, 30–35
Bolivian American, 27
canonical, 30
César Chávez, 25
Christian, 8–9, 12, 13 n. 23, 24, 28, 30–34, 44, 46–47, 49, 79, 86 n. 8, 88, 88 n. 13, 91 n. 18, 92, 95, 97–100
colonial, 26, 26 n. 5, 27–28, 37–38, 45, 67–69, 79, 91, 91 n. 19, 92, 100, 100 n. 48, 106
colonialization, 42
colonialism, 24, 44–45, 83, 91 n. 18
neocolonial, 25, 28, 37, 45
postcolonial, 33 n. 9, 37–38, 42 n. 3, 50 n. 14, 59 n. 22, 68 n. 11, 69 n. 15, 84 n.1, 96 n. 38, 100 n. 48,
community, 3–11, 13–18, 22, 27–31, 34, 37, 41, 43, 43 n. 6, 44, 46–52, 54, 57–58, 61–63, 66–67, 72, 73, 77, 80, 84–85, 87 n. 9, 89, 91, 92 n. 21, 93 n. 24, 94–99, 107, 109–10, 113, 116
Latino/a community, 4–5, 9–10, 13–14, 22, 29–30, 32–34, 37, 39, 44, 52, 57–58, 81, 84, 112–14
constructionist, 28–29
contextual, 22, 27, 29, 31, 46, 59 n. 22, contextualization, 7–12, 16 n. 30, 17
Colombiano/a, 25

Cuban American, 25–27, 33 n. 9, 42, 43 n. 4, 47,
Cubano/a. See Cuban American.
cultural criticism, 4 n. 10, 35–36
difference, 2–3, 3 n. 7, 14, 17–18, 36, 53, 54, 56, 85, 87, 88 n. 12, 89, 94, 100, 104, 107–9, 116
Dolores Huerta, 25
Dominican, 25–27, 47
Dominicano/a. See Dominican.
English, 49, 62, 65–68, 70, 73–74, 76–80, 87 n. 10
English-only, 44, 63, 65
epistemology, 15, 18, 90
essentialism, 24
essentialist, 28–29
ethnography, 30
feminist, 11, 18 n. 32, 31, 84, 113
Fourth Gospel, 16, 41–44, 49, 49 n. 14, 50, 50 n. 15, 51–52, 54–55, 57–59, 61
Galatians, 17, 86–87, 87 n. 10, 88–90, 93–95, 97–100, 100, n. 48, 101, 103, 110
globalization, 44, 66
Guatemalan American, 27
gringo, 66, 66 n. 7
hermeneutics
in general, 1 n. 2, 2, 10
Latin American hermeneutics, 11
Latino/a biblical interpretation, 6–15
as liberation, 11, 30, 38, 46
Hispanic. See Latino/a.
history, 1, 1 n. 2, 5–6, 8–9, 12, 17, 21, 21 n. 1, 23 n. 2, 24, 26, 30, 32 n. 8, 34, 35,

history (cont.)
37, 41, 43, 45, 53, 62, 63 n. 4, 69, 78, 78
n. 38, 79–80, 94–95, 116–117.
as colonialism. *See* colonial: colonialism.
composition, 64
Latin American, 68
redaction, 61 n. 1
reception, 79
US, 63
homogenization, 28
hospitality, 5, 13, 17, 42 n.3, 50, 53, 58,
85–86, 86 nn. 6 and 8, 87, 87 n, 9, 88,
88 n.12, 89, 89 n. 15, 90, 90 n. 16, 91,
91 n. 19, 92, 93, 93 n. 24, 94–95, 95 n.
30, 96, 97, 97 n. 46, 98–99, 110
as ethical, 89, 91 n.19, 92, 92 n. 24, 98
as political, 91, 91 n.19, 92, 100
as colonial, 91, 91 n. 19, 92, 100
hybridity, 33
identity, 5, 8–9, 11, 13–14, 15–16, 16 n.
30, 17–18, 21–23, 23 nn. 2–3, 24–34,
37–39, 45, 47–58, 61 n. 1, 64–67,
71–73, 78, 80–81, 85, 88 n. 10, 89–90,
93, 96–97, 99, 104–6, 106 n. 65, 109,
111–15
as belonging, 14, 14 n. 24, 15
indigenous, 5, 23–24, 28, 42, 46, 67–69
ideological criticism, 31, 35, 37–38
ideology, 14 n. 24, 34–35, 57, 83–84, 84
n. 1
immigration, 23 n. 3, 28, 33, 42 nn. 3, 5,
47, 53
anti-immigration, 44, 52 n. 17
imperial, 12, 27, 31, 45, 47, 68, 73, 73 n.
21, 84, 103
inhospitality, 88–89, 92, 96, 99, 103, 108
intersectionality, 18, 111, 115–16
Jewish, 13 n. 23, 24, 51, 58, 61 n. 1, 91 n.
18, 92, 95, 97, 101, 105–6, 109
journey
as crossing, borders 47
as resettlement, 48–49
as unsettlement, 45–47
Judge Gonzalo P. Curiel, 19 n. 34

globalization, 44, 66
Latin America, 3, 4 n. 8, 11, 23–24, 26–27,
34 n. 10, 38, 42–46, 48, 51, 65–70, 112
Latino/a
as concept, 23–30
Hispanic, 24, n. 4, 25–26
Latinx, 1 n. 1, 18
nomemclature, 1 n. 1, 22, 26, 28
liberation, 12, 13, 19, 30, 38, 46, 84 n. 1,
116
literary criticism, 35–37
Manifest Destiny, 28
marginality, 22, 30–33
Matthew, 72 n. 19, 78
Lord's Prayer, 17, 61–64, 71, 71 n. 18,
72, 74, 79
mestizaje, 46, 46 n. 9,
Mexico, 42 n. 2, 67, 84
Mexican American, 25–27, 42 n. 2, 43, 46
Mexicano/a, 25
migrant, 3, 16, 19 n. 34, 26, n. 5, 43, 47–48
minoritized, 2–3, 10–11, 25, 27 n. 6, 31,
44, 48 n. 13, 85, 116, 117
Monroe Doctrine, 28
Muslim, 24
objectivity, 4, 4 n. 9, 8–9, 27, 36–37, 63
ontology, 18,
Other, 2, n. 4
pedagogical, 16, 63
Protestantism, 24, 37
positivism, 4, 36–37, 46, 63
postcolonial, 37–38, 42, 84
Puerto Rico, 45, 64–66,
Puerto Rican, 25, 27, 45, 45 n. 8, 47,
65, 70 n. 17
Nuyoricans, 25
queer, 18 n. 32
racialization, 3, 48, 83
readers
able-bodied, 18 n. 32
African American, 18 n. 32
Asian, 18 n. 32
disabled-bodied, 18 n. 32
Latina feminist, 18 n. 32
queer, 18 n. 32

CPSIA information can be obtained
at www.ICGtesting.com
Printed in the USA
FSHW010957250621
82669FS